D0856462

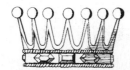

THE RICHTHOFEN FAMILY HERITAGE

Reicht auch der Stammbaum nicht ins graue Altertum,
Ist's dennoch ein gar altes, wackeres Geschlecht;
Christallhell, ungetrübt blieb seines Namens Ruhm,
Hoch hielt es stets die Wahrheit, Ehre und das Recht.
Treu seiner Väter Brauch, fromm, tapfer, brav und schlicht,
Hat Gottes gnäd'ge Huld vor Schaden es bewahrt.
O wank auch fürder nicht vom Pfad der Christenpflicht,
Führ deinen Namen stolz nach echter Ritterart!
Es blühe mächtig dies Geschlecht, der Ehre Bild,
Nie fall' ein Schatten auf sein Wappenschild!

Reaching back not into grey antiquity, the family tree
Is nevertheless of an indeed old and worthy lineage;
Crystal-clear, unclouded remains the glory of its name,
Held high for all time in truth, honour and justice.
True to ancestral ways, devout, brave, honest and modest,
Has by God's gracious favour been protected from harm.
Oh, waver not from the path of Christian duty,
Further your name proudly in the manner of true knights!
Even as the lineage flowers heartily, the very picture of honour,
Never shall a shadow fall upon this noble escutcheon!

Verses that serve as the motto of the history of the Richthofen
family, composed by the German envoy, Emil Freiherr von
Richthofen, who died in 1895. New translation by Peter Kilduff
and new rendering of the Richthofen crest by Greg VanWyngarden.

THE ILLUSTRATED
RED BARON

The Life and Times of
Manfred von Richthofen

PETER KILDUFF

ARMS AND
ARMOUR

This book is dedicated to Falk Hallensleben,
who has worked with singular devotion to preserve
the history of the Richthofen Geschwader
from its beginning to the present.

Arms and Armour
An Imprint of the Cassell Group
Wellington House, 125 Strand,
London WC2R 0BB

940.4
4943
Kild

First published 1999

British Library Cataloguing-in-Publication Data:
a catalogue record for this book is available from
the British Library

ISBN 1-85409-414-9

Distributed in the USA by Sterling Publishing Co.
Inc., 387 Park Avenue South, New York,
NY 10016-8810.

Designed and edited by DAG Publications Ltd.
Designed by David Gibbons; edited by Michael
Boxall; layout by Anthony A. Evans; printed and
bound in Great Britain.

Also by Peter Kilduff

The Red Baron
That's My Bloody Plane
Germany's Last Knight of the Air
US Carriers at War
A-4 Skyhawk
Germany's First Air Force 1914–1918
Richthofen – Beyond the Legend of the Red Baron
Over the Battlefronts
The Red Baron Combat Wing

Contents

Foreword

It is quite remarkable that my uncle Manfred was remembered by the present-day Jagdgeschwader Richthofen in Wittmund, East Frisia, on 21 April 1998, the 80th anniversary of his death. A large delegation from the present Geschwader assembled in the Wittmund market square. The Luftwaffe Music Corps provided musical accompaniment. Many hundreds of citizens gathered, together with the soldiers, in order to remember this air force officer of the First World War.

This event followed by some years – and only after lengthy negotiations with the then German Democratic Republic regime – the success of my father, Bolko Freiherr von Richthofen, in having Manfred's grave, his mortal remains and the memorial stone brought to Wiesbaden for a fitting interment in 1976. His grave in the *Invalidenfriedhof* (Cemetery for the Disabled) in East Berlin had been completely neglected. It had not been possible to care for the grave because the cemetery had been located within an off-limits area of the GDR's intra-German border.

My grandmother, Kunigunde Freifrau von Richthofen, died in 1962 and she was buried in Wiesbaden. Following her escape from the family home in Schweidnitz, Silesia, she had found a new home there and lived for some time with her daughter Ilse von Reibnitz (née Richthofen). A large gravesite was acquired for the mortal remains of my grandmother, my uncle Manfred, my aunt Ilse and my father Bolko, who was Manfred's youngest brother. After my uncle was re-interred in Wiesbaden, my father donated the *Invalidenfriedhof* memorial stone to the Geschwader in Wittmund, where it now occupies a place of honour.

Incidentally, Bolko, who was the only family member not to become a professional soldier, but a successful businessman, also honoured the family tradition and maintained ties to active duty pilots. For this he received honours from the Royal Canadian Air Force, was awarded the title 'Honorary Commander' by the Americans, and was always a welcome guest with NATO air units. My father attempted to reclaim for the family the Richthofen Museum in Schweidnitz, a collection of 'Red Baron' mementoes, which had been carried off by the Russians during the conquest of Silesia. We know that the contents of the museum were taken to Moscow. The former Soviet regime employed delaying tactics in replying to letters to Josef Stalin from my grandmother and father, requesting the return of a few personal memorabilia of the famous sons. Today my family is still trying to obtain these from the current Russian government.

It is somewhat surprising that new photographs of my uncle's life as a pilot continue to surface. They include documentation of his burial at the *Invalidenfriedhof* and countless photographs taken by many men, women and young people during his appearances at schools, hospitals and nursing homes. Even the keepers of the Tradition Room at Jagdgeschwader Richthofen continue to receive mail every month from around the world concerning the 'Red Baron' phenomenon.

This book bears impressive witness to the fact that, thanks to photography, which has undergone such lightning-swift development during the 20th century, we are able to see new aspects of historic personalities and events. Through many previously unknown photographs this book presents a new and more extensive insight into the life of Rittmeister Manfred von Richthofen, as well as providing dramatic glimpses of the world of early aviation.

Manfred von Richthofen
Berlin, Germany, May 1998

Introduction

Of all the aviation heroes of the First World War, Manfred von Richthofen has gained a special place in the history of that era. First and foremost, the young nobleman – a hereditary *Freiherr* (Baron) – evoked a modern image of a gallant aristocrat assuming the combat leadership role that went with his rank in society. His fulfilment of *noblesse oblige* came when Rittmeister (Cavalry Captain) von Richthofen became the war's top-scoring fighter pilot. He shot down 80 enemy aircraft.

The second reason for his lasting fame is that Manfred von Richthofen was a bold and fearless aerial combatant, a capable and charismatic leader who earned the trust of his superiors and had an almost mystical ability to inspire his men to emulate his bravery and achievements. He was the star pupil of the great airfighter Hauptmann (Army Captain) Oswald Boelcke and went on to command his own Jagdstaffel (Fighter Aircraft Section) and then to lead Germany's first Jagdgeschwader (Fighter Air Wing).

Third, Manfred von Richthofen became and remains a character of 20th-century mass communication media; he had a natural ability to look good for still or motion picture cameras and had personal charm to impress journalists and other civilians who met him. Athletic and handsome, Manfred von Richthofen projected what is now called

'star quality', an important asset to the German military administration that needed to cultivate popular heroes to reinforce public support for a protracted and debilitating war.

To affirm the correctness of its own role in furthering the air hero's image, the German press eagerly reprinted a neutral newspaper's report which mirrored their own impressions. A Dutch journalist who visited Richthofen at the Front in early May 1917 found him to be '... a young man of at most 25 years of age, with bright blue eyes that revealed a good nature and a cheerful smile.

'What could he really tell me? [That he had] flown for only a short time. He'd had good luck. The German aeroplanes now in use are not inferior to the French and British [aircraft]. Also the German pilots

are not lacking in boldness. And that his Geschwader had just been especially lucky – it had brought down 140 enemies, while only two members of his Staffel had not returned – and, Richthofen himself wrote, on the whole, the German flyers were better marksmen. But all had high regard for the British flers, (who were) courageous fellows and tough sportsmen who, for all that, regarded flying not only as a sport, but also as a science. As opponents, they are to be taken more seriously than the French, who, to be sure, did not lack courage and confidence, but who counted too much on their elegant fighting style.

'The young Rittmeister told all about it without boasting. A man who in hundreds of aerial engagements had come to know mortal danger is indeed fully conscious of his glory; he knows, however, that the fatal moment that did not spare Boelcke and Immelmann can also come for him. He who must stand ready, night and day, to undertake the dangerous hazards of war, as young and famous as he may be, has no sympathy for boasting. His nerves are like the bracing wires of his aeroplane, sturdy and ever taut. His jaw remains firm, his appearance calm.'[1]

The same public mood that embraced the wartime image of Manfred von Richthofen later accepted the portrayal of First World War aerial combats created in the photographs of the Cockburn-Lange Collection, on the preceding page and below left. Despite the availability of actual air-to-air photographs, such as the one above and on the following pages, the Cockburn-Lange photos were not proved to be fraudulent until some 70 years after the war.[2] The photographic images of Manfred von Richthofen are genuine, but they also merit closer examination by the modern world.

While gathering material for a translation of Manfred von Richthofen's memoirs, a biography and an operational history of the air wing he led, the author has viewed thousands of photographs pertaining to the 'Red Baron' and his era. The present work presents newly found material and information not used in my previous books and tells more of the story with some of the media that used, and were skilfully used by, Richthofen.

This book would not have been possible without help from friends, colleagues and organisations over many years. Special thanks are extended to: the late Wing Commander Ronald Adam, OBE; F. W. Bailey; Gottfried Baron; Dr. Friedrich R.

sarchiv Gotha; Traditions-Gemeinschaft 'Alte Adler' (Germany); University of Texas at Dallas; US National Archives (Washington, D.C.); Wehrgeschichtliches Museum (Rastatt).

The author is grateful to Dr. Hermann Freiherr von Richthofen, Germany's Permanent Representative to NATO, and Manfred Freiherr von Richthofen, nephew and namesake of the renowned *Rittmeister*, for their interest and encouragement in the development of this book.

Special thanks go to friends

Bechtle; the late Dr. Gustav Bock; the family of the late General der Flieger a.D. Karl Bodenschatz; Dr. Kees Booij; Charles H. Donald; the late A. E. Ferko; Dr. Erich Fritsch; Dr. Achim Fuchs; Peter M. Grosz; Dr. Emmanuel Gustin; Falk Hallensleben; Janice Hayzlett; Dr. Volker Koos; the late Clayton Knight, OBE; Prof. Dr. Zdzislaw Kremens; Lt Col. John Moncure, US Army (Ret); Dr.-Ing. Albert Niedermeyer; Neal W. O'Connor; Fritzcarl Prestien; Julian Putkowski; the late Oberstleutnant der Reserve a.D. Hanns-Gerd Rabe; Dr. Hans-Jörg Ruge; Dr. Larry D. Sall; Dr. Leroy Temple; Lothair Vanoverbeke; Greg VanWyngarden; George H. Williams, Jr.; Dr. Jürgen Willisch and Dr. Erdmann Zimmer-Vorhaus.

The author greatly appreciates help received from these institutions: Bayerisches Hauptstaatsarchiv (Munich); Belgian Army Museum (Brussels); Bundesarchiv Militärarchiv (Freiburg); Elihu Burritt Library of Central Connecticut State University (New Britain); Generallandesarchiv Karlsruhe; Hauptstaatsarchiv Stuttgart; Imperial War Museum (London); Luftwaffenmuseum der Bundeswehr (Berlin-Gatow); Jagdgeschwader 71 of the Luftwaffe (Wittmund); Militärisches Museum der Bundeswehr (Dresden); National Aviation Museum of Canada (Ottawa); Public Record Office (London); Technical University of Wroclaw (Poland); Thüringisches Staat-

who helped in various unseen ways: Roderick Dymott and Karl Eckert for listening to ideas as the book took shape; David Gibbons of DAG Publications Ltd. for creating the attractive layout and typography that weaves together these words and photographs; Dena Harwin for proofreading the text and Dr. S. Martin Harwin for being so helpful in preparing photographs; and Gary Warner, whose computer expertise ensured that modern technology served fully in assembling this material.

As always, special thanks go to my wife, Judy, for keeping things going on the home front while I was spending many hours in archives or in thought for this book.

Finally, out of profound respect for the combatants of all nations who perished or were captured or wounded during the First World War, the author has chronicled as many of their names as possible in the endnotes. To keep the process relevant but concise, the following abbreviations have been used to indicate what happened to them: EA (Enemy Aircraft); KiA (killed in action); KiC (killed in crash); WiA (wounded in action); DoW (died of wounds); PoW (prisoner of war) .

Peter Kilduff
New Britain, Connecticut
July 1998

1 — The Legend Begins

Below: Manfred Albrecht Freiherr von Richthofen lived for 9,486 days. In that time he rose from being an obscure cavalry officer of no great promise to become Imperial Germany's most successful fighter pilot, squadron leader and wing commander. He was credited with shooting down 80 enemy aeroplanes during 20 months in combat over the Western Front and received 24 military decorations, thereby becoming Germany's most highly decorated aviator of the war.[1] His value to his nation's wartime propa-

ganda effort is seen in the first of many popular postcards of the day to bear his likeness. This card, the only one in the series showing him in full dress uniform, describes Richthofen as being 'our most successful combat airman'. It appeared after his stunning successes in April 1917, during which he shot down 21 aeroplanes and raised his score to 52. At his collar is the blue enamel and gold Maltese cross of the *Orden Pour le Mérite*, Prussia's highest award for bravery. Below it are: the Iron Cross 1st Class; Knight's Cross with Swords of the Royal Order of the House of Hohenzollern; Duke Eduard Carl Medal with Date Clasp and Swords, awarded by the Duchy of Saxe–Coburg–Gotha; Austro–Hungarian Empire's Military Merit Cross 3rd Class with War Decoration.

Opposite page, top: Richthofen shot down 60 enemy aeroplanes while flying Albatros biplane fighters. On its introduction in mid-1916, the Albatros series' 'rugged strength and careful attention to streamlining'[2] gave him and his contemporaries the first-rate fighter needed to compete with numerically superior British and French air forces. Seen here is a machine reported to be Albatros D.V 2059/17, the only aeroplane actually flown by Richthofen to survive the First World War.[3] As with many physical remnants of his airfighting career, this all-red Albatros helped perpetuate the Richthofen legend between the wars when it was displayed in the Zeughaus (Armoury) in Berlin. It was destroyed in an Allied bombing raid during the Second World War.

Opposite page, bottom: The Richthofen family can be traced back to the Middle Ages. One ancestor, Johann Praetorius (1611–64), rose to the hereditary

Bohemian Knighthood in 1661, and his Latin-root family name was Germanised to Richthofen (court of judgement). In 1741, King Friedrich II of Prussia (Frederick the Great) elevated the family to the baronial ranks, granting male members the hereditary title *Freiherr* and women the title *Freifrau*. The family produced leaders in civic, educational and military endeavours. As expected, the three male children of career army officer Albrecht Philip Karl Julius von Richthofen (1859-1920) followed him into the Prussian military system. They are from left: Karl Bolko, born 16 April 1903; Manfred Albrecht, born 2 May 1892; and Lothar Siegfried, born 27 September 1894. The two elder sons and a daughter, Elisabeth Therese Luise Marie (called Ilse), were born in Breslau, Lower Silesia. Karl Bolko was born in Schweidnitz, where this photograph was taken while Manfred was on holiday leave from the Cadet Institute at Wahlstatt (now Legnicke Pole, Poland). Of Albrecht's influence on his childhood, Manfred wrote: 'The old gentleman was assigned to [the mounted unit] Leib-Kürassier-Regiment Nr. 1 in Breslau when I was born ... I had private tutors until my ninth year of life, then a year of public school in Schweidnitz, [and] later I became a cadet.'[4]

Below: Manfred von Richthofen's military career, which began at the age of 11, was typical of young men of his generation. 'I was not overly fond of becoming a cadet, but it was my father's wish and I was little consulted about it,' he wrote later. 'The strict discipline and order was hard on such a young pup [and] I did not care very much for the instruction. I was never a great scholar... [However] all risky tricks impressed me mightily. So, one fine day my friend Frankenberg and I climbed the well-known church steeple of Wahlstatt by going up the lightning rod. I tied my handkerchief to the top of the steeple ... I saw my handkerchief still tied high in the air ten years later when I visited my little brother Bolko at Wahlstatt.'[5] Manfred persevered and went on to the Main Cadet Institute at Gross-Lichterfelde, outside Berlin, but not without some personal cost. A passing remark in his autobiography alluded to some physical or psychological pain endured during those formative years: 'Actually, I can say little about my military school time. It reminded me very much of the cadet corps and, because of that, is not too pleasant a memory.'[6] It also demonstrated his ability to compartmentalise his feelings, a useful trait in the

crucible of war. In this picture from 1912, unpleasant memories seem to have faded in comparison to the glow of Manfred's new uniform as a *Fähnrich* (Ensign) in Ulanen-Regiment Nr. 1.

Above: At the beginning of the war Manfred was a Leutnant (Second Lieutenant) serving on the German border with Russian-occupied Poland. It was too calm a sector for a young warrior eager for combat and he was elated when his regiment was ordered to the Western Front. As his unit advanced, Manfred felt the personal side of war when his 24-year-old cousin Wolfram was killed by a Belgian sharpshooter on 11 August.[7] Eleven days later, in the thick of the fighting for Virton, Richthofen's former cadet comrade, Leutnant Helmut von Frankenberg und Ludwigsdorf, was killed.[8] After adjusting to these realities, Manfred chafed at the boredom that set in after the first few months of war. Like the rider in the photograph, he learned that wrecked cities and mud-filled trenches thwart the cavalryman's mobility. His frustration gave way to impetuosity when he was assigned mundane tasks as an orderly officer, and he took direct action: 'Now I wrote to the sector commanding general and malicious tongues contend that I said: "Dear Excellency, I did not go to war to gather cheese and eggs, but, rather, for another purpose." At first people took offence at my request, but finally it was granted and so at the end of May 1915 I joined the Fliegertruppe [Flying Service]. Thus was my greatest wish fulfilled.'[9]

Above: Two-seat reconnaissance aeroplanes, such as this Albatros B.II, gained added importance when barbed wire and trench emplacements obstructed the traditional cavalry mission of reconnoitring the forward lines and beyond. To fill that intelligence-gathering gap, many German officers were trained as aviation observers who directed their enlisted pilots, as if they were aeroplane 'drivers', to transport them over the lines. Thus, Manfred was assigned to the aviation training unit Flieger-Ersatz-Abteilung 7 in Cologne to become an observer. His description of his first flight reflects some initial perplexity in the new role: 'We drove to the airfield, [where] I sat in an aeroplane for the first time. The wind-blast from the propeller annoyed me tremendously. It was not possible for me to communicate with the pilot. Everything flew away from me. If I took out a piece of paper, it disappeared. My flying helmet slipped off, my muffler loosened too much and the jacket was not buttoned securely – in short, it was miserable. Before I knew what was happening, the pilot got the engine up to full speed and the machine began rolling. Ever faster, ever faster. I hung on frantically. All of a sudden the shaking stopped and the machine was in the air. The ground slipped away beneath me.'[10]

Right: When Richthofen posed for this photograph in Cologne on 1 May 1917, his days as a neophyte student observer were two years behind him. But it must have given him personal satisfaction to stand

before an Albatros trainer similar to the one in which he had made his first flights. The 52-victory ace and *Pour le Mérite* recipient was on his way to meet Kaiser Wilhelm II the following day. Richthofen's luncheon appointment with the Supreme Warlord also fell on his own 25th (and last) birthday, after which he went home to Schweidnitz to work on his memoirs. Surely, the exhilaration of those early days was clearly in mind when he wrote: 'We flew straight ahead for a

bit, then my pilot turned and turned again, first to the right, then to the left, and I lost my orientation to the airfield. I no longer had any idea where I was! Cautiously I began to look over the side at the region below. The people looked tiny, [and] the houses as if they were from a child's toybox, everything was so small and fine. In the background lay Cologne. The Kölner Dom [Cathedral] looked like a plaything. It was a glorious feeling to sail over everything. Who could touch me now? No one! I did not care that I no longer knew where I was, and I was quite sad when my pilot said that we had to land now.'[11]

Below: After little more than a month at FEA 7 in Albatros two-seaters of the type seen here, and another accelerated aviation course at FEA 6 in Grossenhain in Saxony, Richthofen was posted to Feldflieger-Abteilung 69 on the Eastern Front. He recalled: 'Of course, I wanted to get right out there, for I was afraid that I would be too late to take part in the World War. It would have taken three months to qualify as a pilot. By then we could have been long at peace; therefore that option did not come into question. In my capacity as a cavalryman perhaps I would be well suited as an observer; for after fourteen days [of training] I was sent out, to my great joy, to the one place where there was still mobile warfare, namely to Russia.'[12] He was not disappointed. Feld-

flieger-Abteilung 69 was a very active unit, assigned first to reconnoitre an extensive area of the Front held by German 11. Armee and then shifted to an expanse covered by Austro–Hungarian 6. Armeekorps. Best of all, Richthofen was paired with a pilot eager for action, Oberleutnant Georg Zeumer. When Zeumer was shifted to Flanders to rejoin his old unit, the *Brieftauben-Abteilung* (Carrier Pigeon Section) in Ostend, Richthofen flew with Rittmeister Erich Graf von Holck, another daring pilot. For more about Zeumer and Holck, see Appendix I.

Right: As an observer, Manfred gained first-hand knowledge about 'backseat flyers' which helped him become a more proficient fighter pilot. For example, he recognised that the two-gun battle station in the Albatros (shown here) enhanced the observer's firepower, but put him at greater personal risk. Richthofen's brief air combat operations manual, compiled near the end of his life and based on his varied experiences, noted: 'One attacks the two-seater from behind at great speed, in the same direction he is going. The only way to avoid the adroit observer's field of machine-gun fire is to stay calm and put the observer out of action with the first shots. If the opponent goes into a turn, I must be careful not to fly above the enemy aeroplane. A long aerial combat with a completely combat-ready, manoeuvrable two-seater is the most difficult ... I consider it to be very dangerous to attack a two-seater from the front. In the first place, one seldom encounters the opponent [this way]. On the contrary, first of all I am within the field of fire of his fixed [forward-firing] machine-gun, and then in the observer's [wider field of fire]. If I squeeze through below the two-seater and then want to make a turn, while in the turns I offer the [enemy] observer the best target.'[13]

of the German General Staff, who would be helpful when he rose to command level. For the time being he had to master the two-engined AEG G.I bomber (seen here), with which the clumsily cover-named Carrier Pigeon Section carried out raids behind enemy lines. He and Zeumer experienced difficult flights, as on an occasion over the English Channel when, he wrote: ' ... suddenly I noticed that water was disappearing from one of

Below: 'After our ventures in Russia gradually came to a halt, suddenly, on 21 August 1915, I was transferred to fly a "*Grosskampfflugzeug*" [big battle 'plane] at the *Brieftauben-Abteilung* Ostend. There I met my old friend Zeumer ...', Richthofen wrote of his abrupt shift back to the Western Front. Once again his good luck held and he received a choice assignment, working with top people such as Leutnant Fritz von Falkenhayn, son of the former Chief

our radiators. I did not like that very much and I brought it to his attention. He made a long face and prepared to return home. But we were roughly 20 kilometres off the coast and first we had to fly that far. The engine began to quit and I quietly prepared myself for a cold bath. But behold, it went on! The giant apple-barge managed with one engine and the excellent new steering rod, and we reached the coast and made a beautiful landing at our airfield.'[14]

Right: Manfred von Richthofen had special reason to remember AEG G.I bombers, because he received his first combat-related injury in one. As this photograph of a Carrier Pigeon Section aeroplane shows, the position of the wings made it difficult for AEG G.I crews to look downward at their targets. On one occasion during a flight over British lines Richthofen found a simple solution: 'When the bomb explodes below and one sees the lovely grey-white cloud of the explosion and that it is close to the target, it gives one much joy. So I signalled to my good Zeumer to fly [at a steep angle] so that the wings were off to the side. In so doing I forgot that the infamous thing, my apple-barge, had two propellers, which turned to the right and left near my observer's seat. I was showing him about where the bomb hit and – smack! – one of my fingers was struck. Somewhat startled at first, I determined that my little finger had been injured. Zeumer noticed nothing. I was sick of dropping bombs, quickly let the last ones go and we made our way home. My love for the big battle 'plane, which in any case was a bit weak, suffered from this bombing mission. I had to stay behind and not fly

for eight days. Now my finger has only a blemish, but at least I can say with pride: "I, too, have a war wound."'[15]

Opposite page, bottom: The *Brieftauben-Abteilung* Ostend was the mobile aerial strike force of its day. On short notice, BAO crews could be off to a new sector in their own train. Richthofen described how his ambitions were bolstered during an encounter with the notable fighter pilot Oswald Boelcke (see Appendix I) in a BAO railway car like the one seen here: 'We were assembled into a Combat Air Wing and headed out [to the Champagne Sector by train] on 1 October 1915. In the dining-car, a young unpretentious Leutnant sat at the next table. There was no reason to take special notice of him except for one fact: of all of us he was the only one who had shot down an enemy airman and, indeed, it was not just one, but four. He had been mentioned by name in the Army Daily Report ... Although I had made great efforts, up until then I had not bagged one ... [and] ... I wanted very much to learn how this Leutnant Boelcke had done it. So I asked him: "Tell me honestly, how do you really do it?" He laughed, greatly amused, even though I really asked seriously. Then he answered: "Yes, good heavens, it is quite simple. I fly right up to [the enemy], take good aim [and open fire], and then he falls down."'[16]

Below: Richthofen was quick to realise that an observer in twin-engined bombers could not become an aerial combatant like Boelcke. 'So I came to the decision: "You must learn to fly a Fokker yourself, then perhaps things will be better",' he wrote. 'Now my thoughts and aspirations were on how to learn to "work the stick" myself.'[17] His later success derived from an incident that occurred at the time he left the cavalry. On 18 April 1915, the French fighter pilot Roland Garros was forced down in this Morane-Saulnier Type L parasol monoplane and German technicians learned how he had been able to shoot down aeroplanes by firing his machine-gun through the propeller arc. Garros had steel wedges fitted to the propeller blades to deflect bullets that did not pass through the arc. The crude device was turned over to the aeroplane designer Anthony Fokker (see Appendix I), whose engineers developed a more effective push-rod gear which interrupted the machine-gun's firing sequence when the propeller blade was in front of the muzzle. This refinement helped Leutnant Oswald Boelcke become a major airfighter in Fokker monoplanes. In November 1915, Manfred von Richthofen began pilot training at Döberitz, outside Berlin – the same facility where Garros' captured aeroplane had been evaluated.

Above: While he was with Feldflieger-Abteilung 69, Manfred von Richthofen had qualified for the *Beobachterabzeichen* (Observer's Badge) although no surviving photographs show him wearing it. The badge was established by Imperial Decree on the last pre-war birthday of Kaiser Wilhelm II, 27 January 1914, and was awarded only to officers.[18] As an observer, Richthofen was nominally in charge of the aeroplane, but that applied only if he flew with an enlisted pilot. Most of his early flights were with officers who outranked him and his status as a 'passenger' or simply an aerial gunner may have added to his desire to become a pilot and to fly single-seat fighters, of which he would have complete control.

Above right: An Imperial Decree of exactly one year earlier established the *Flugzeugführerabzeichen* (Pilot's Badge), which was awarded to 'officers, non-commissioned officers and other ranks who had earned it after passing written tests and after completing their training at a military air station and receiving a qualifying certificate as a military aeroplane pilot'.[19] As he recounted, Richthofen almost

ended his career on his first solo flight: 'I started the engine, gave it the gas, and the machine began to pick up speed. All of a sudden I could not help but notice that I was really flying. At last it was not an anxious but, rather, a daring feeling. Now it was all up to me. Come what may, I was no longer frightened. With contempt for death I made a wide left turn, turned off the engine precisely over the designated tree and waited to see what would happen. Then came the most difficult part, the landing. I remembered precisely the essential movements of the controls. I performed them mechanically, however, and the machine responded differently from when [Georg] Zeumer sat at the controls. I lost my equilibrium, made some wrong movements and landed the training machine on its nose. Very sadly I surveyed the damage, which, luckily, was not extensive ... [and] two days later I went back to my aeroplane with mad passion and everything went wonderfully well.'[20]

Opposite page, top: Following pilot training, Richthofen flew Albatros two-seaters with Kampf-staffel 8 of Kampfgeschwader 2 over the Verdun

sector. He seems subdued here in conversation with Kasta 8's commanding officer, Hauptmann Victor Carganico (left), a pre-war military aviator and BAO veteran. The mood may have matched that when Richthofen's victory of 16 April 1916 was acknowledged but, as he noted, not credited to him: ' ... I had a machine-gun mounted between the wings of my machine [outside the propeller arc], just like the Nieuport, and was very proud of this construction. Some people laughed at it because it looked very primitive ... [but] soon I had the opportunity to use it in a practical way [when] I encountered a Nieuport which, apparently, was also flown by a beginner, for he acted foolishly fearful ... I flew after him and for the first time, from an ever-closing distance, pressed the firing button of the machine-gun; a short series of well-aimed shots and the Nieu-

port reared up and rolled over. At first my observer and I thought it was one of the many tricks the Frenchmen like to pull. But this trick did not stop; he went down lower and lower ... [and] fell in a forest behind Fort Douaumont ... on the other side ... A day later I read of my heroic deed in the Army Report. I was not unduly proud of it, but this Nieuport is not counted among my 52 [victories].'[21]

Below: 'From the beginning of my career as a pilot I had only one aspiration and that was to ... fly a single-seat fighter plane,' Richthofen wrote. 'After a long annoyance to my commanding officer, I wangled permission to go up in a Fokker. The rotary engine revolving with the propeller [bolted to it] was entirely new to me. Also, sitting by myself in a small aeroplane was strange to me.'[22] Richthofen scored no victories while flying Fokker Eindeckers (monoplanes), but he gained his initial experience in the aeroplane type in which he would become most successful. This view of a Fokker Eindecker cockpit shows the sparse instrumentation, steering column with built-in machine-gun firing controls and tight space that kept man and machine in such intimate contact that the aeroplane became an extension of the pilot as he engaged in the oldest mode of warfare: individual combat.

Above: In addition to Oswald Boelcke, the other high-scoring Fokker Eindecker pilot was Oberleutnant Max Immelmann (see Appendix I). One of the aeroplanes that he flew – Fokker E 3/15 seen here – survived the First World War and was displayed in the Saxon Army Museum in Dresden, only to be destroyed during the Second World War. These early models were passed along to fledgling pilots such as Richthofen and for good reason, as he wrote about the Eindecker he shared with Leutnant Hans Reimann: 'I flew it in the morning, [and] he in the afternoon. Each was afraid the other would smash

the crate. [One day] we flew against the enemy. In the morning I encountered no Frenchmen, but in the afternoon it was a different story [when Reimann flew]. He did not return, there was no report, nothing. Late that evening the infantry reported a combat between a Nieuport and a Fokker, after the German had apparently landed on the other side ... It could only have been Reimann, for all of the others had returned. We were feeling sorry for our courageous comrade when suddenly that night came a telephone report that a German officer pilot had appeared in the forward-most infantry position ... It turned out to be Reimann ... Some weeks later we received a second Fokker. This time I felt obligated to dispatch it to the hereafter ...'[23]

Left: Manfred wrote to his mother that on the morning of 2 May 1916, his 24th birthday, he 'had three very nerve-wracking aerial combats' over the Verdun sector. All without success. In the same letter he commented on his new duties as a fighter pilot and about a friend's fate that he would share two weeks before his own 26th birthday: 'I feel very content in my new occupation as a combat airman; I believe that no post in the war is as attractive as this one. I fly a Fokker, which is the aeroplane with which Boelcke and Immelmann have had their enormous successes. I am very sorry about the death of [Rittmeister Erich Graf von] Holck. I visited him three days before he fell and we had a good time together ... I was an eye-witness to his last air battle. First he shot down a Frenchman from a large formation, then apparently had a gun-jam and wanted to fly back over our lines. Then a whole swarm of Frenchmen pounced on him. With a shot

Ein von Leutnant Immelmann heruntergeschossenes französisches Flugzeug.

through the head, he tumbled down from 3,000 metres. A beautiful death. Holck with only one arm or one leg would be unimaginable. Today I fly to his funeral.'[24]

Above: To ensure that Oberleutnant Max Immelmann's victories inspired other airmen, as well as the general public, the ace's exploits were widely publicised. His fourth combat success was the subject of this illustrated postcard. On the afternoon of 10 October 1915, while flying between Lens and Loos – territory that would become familiar to Richthofen just over a year later – Immelmann shot down B.E.2c 2033 of No. 16 Squadron, RFC. Firing some 400 shots at the British two-seater, Immelmann caused it to crash into a stand of trees. He visited the crash site and later described a scene that presaged the recognition accorded to Richthofen: 'The pilot died a short time later, as he had been shot six times, and the observer had a slight leg wound. The aeroplane was completely destroyed. At the outset I had rendered the machine-gun useless with a shot to the breech. While I was still at the scene, Prince Ernst Heinrich of Saxony arrived; he wanted to know all about what had happened and, finally, invited me to dinner.'[25]

Right: When Immelmann was killed while flying a Fokker Eindecker, his death was one of several notable casualties that shook the German Flying Service in June 1916. Then Germany's second highest-scoring fighter ace, Immelmann was engaging a British two-seater when he fell under unexplained circumstances on the 18th. The next day, prominent air wing commander Hauptmann Ernst Freiherr von Gersdorff was killed when his Fokker was shot down by a French fighter. Two days later, a Frenchman killed Oberleutnant Hans Bailer, commander of the air wing in which Manfred's brother Lothar was serving. Fokker's aeroplanes and the tactics of Boelcke and Immelmann had secured German aerial superiority, but new British and French pilots and aeroplanes were turning the tables. Manfred von Richthofen's worried look in this photograph from his KG 2 days is matched by the haunting question and sombre tone of his letter of 22 June: 'What do you think of Immelmann's death? In the long run everyone believes it. Even Boelcke. The commander of Lothar's combat air wing

has also not returned from a bombing mission. A day before that the commander of my old KG 1, formerly the BAO, was also shot down. He was Freiherr von Gersdorff, easily the most qualified commander a combat air wing commander ever had. I always liked him very much.'[26]

Opposite page, bottom: In early July, Manfred crashed in his Fokker Eindecker and emerged from the tangled wreckage unhurt. He considered writing to Boelcke and asking to join his unit, but was too late. Aware of the morale value of its heroes, the German High Command avoided the risk of losing another top pilot so soon after Immelmann's death by sending Boelcke on a good-will tour to Turkey. At the same time, KG 2 went to Russia, where activities provided enough good memories for Richthofen's later reflection, as can be seen here with Hauptmann Victor Carganico (second from left) and Leutnant Alfred Gerstenberg (right). Richthofen recalled: 'We travelled through all of Germany in our railway living

quarters consisting of dining- and sleeping-cars and, at last, came to Kovel. There we stayed on our train. This business of living on trains has many advantages, of course. One is always ready to travel on and always has the same living-quarters. But in the Russian summer heat, a sleeping-car is the most dreadful thing there is. For that reason, I decided to go with two good friends, Gerstenberg and [Franz Christian von] Scheele into a nearby forest, where we pitched a tent and lived like gypsies. Those were lovely times.'[27]

Below: Richthofen was back flying one of the Albatros C.IIIs in the line-up seen here during a visit to Kampfgeschwader 2 by Prince Leopold of Bavaria (A). Another KG 2 pilot, Leutnant der Reserve Erwin Böhme, recalled: 'From 15 to 23 July 1916 our Geschwader was with the [9.] Armee commanded by Prince Leopold. The old gentleman was enormously interested in aviation and wanted to fly over the Front with us himself. But, due to almost continuous

rain during the whole time, altogether we got to fly twice.'[28] While inspecting the unit, the Prince spoke with some of the young officers. Here, he addresses Leutnants Manfred von Richthofen (B) and Alfred Gerstenberg. Richthofen did not record what he said to KG 2's distinguished visitor, but he did note his own perception of the pace of the war: 'Compared to the Western Front, in any case, flying on the Eastern Front is relaxation ... We have time and no one bothers us. An enemy airfield is right in the area, but its pilots are not to be seen. Anti-aircraft shells burst sporadically and in quite another direction from the one we are flying.'[29]

Below: A taste of things to come was this KG 2 celebration in honour of Oberleutnant Oswald Boelcke (seated, right) when he visited the Geschwader at Mont in France in March 1916. Almost six months later he established the fighter section Jagdstaffel 2 and three pilots at this party were among those he selected: Leutnant der Reserve Erwin Böhme (standing behind Boelcke); Leutnant der Reserve Hans Imelmann (seated); Leutnant der Reserve Hans Wortmann (standing behind Imelmann). Boelcke also chose Manfred von Richthofen. 'We were talking among ourselves when someone said: "Today the great Boelcke is coming and wants to visit us or, rather, his brother in Kovel,"' Richthofen wrote. 'That evening the famous man appeared, very impressively to us, and told us many interesting things about his journey to Turkey, whence he was on the way back, to report to Supreme Headquarters. He talked about going to the Somme sector to carry on his work; also he was to set up an entire Jagdstaffel. For this purpose he could select from the Flying Service people who appeared to him to be suitable. I dared not ask him to take me with him. Not on the basis that our air wing had become too boring for me – on the contrary, we made extensive and interesting flights and pounded many a Russki railway station with our bombs – but the thought of fighting again on the Western Front appealed to me. There is nothing finer for a young cavalry officer than to fly off to the chase.'[30] Next morning, Boelcke appeared at Richthofen's quarters and invited him to join Jasta 2. Three days later Richthofen went home on leave and then on to France. As he departed KG 2, a friend called out: 'Don't come back without the *Pour le Mérite!*' In less than five months Manfred von Richthofen became the fourteenth fighter pilot to receive that coveted award.'[31]

2 — One Eagle Falls, Another Rises

Right: Hauptmann Oswald Boelcke's return to the Western Front was marked by new airfighting triumphs. On 2 September 1916 he was credited with victory No. 20 and within two months he doubled that score. Aircraft designer and manufacturer Anthony Fokker wanted Boelcke and his comrades to fly the new biplane fighters, such as the Fokker

D.II seen here, and for a brief time Jagdstaffel 2 was successful with them. Boelcke wrote on 4 September: 'A few days ago two machines arrived from Fokker for me and the day before yesterday I made my first flight [in one of them]. At the Front there was quite a lot of enemy air activity. The lads [on the other side] have become very bold ... A bit later I saw shellbursts west of Puisieux. There I found a B.E. biplane and behind him three Vickers [*sic*] single-seaters: an artillery-spotting aeroplane and its escorts. I went

after the B.E. But in the middle of my work, the three others interrupted me, whereupon I promptly withdrew. One of these lads ... came after me. Slightly away from the others I began battling with him and soon had him all wrapped up. I did not let him get away and he fired no more shots. While going down he wobbled violently and quite involuntarily, as he said afterwards, because his elevator cables had been shot through. He came down north-east of Thiepval.'[1]

Left: Boelcke inspects his 24th victim, an Airco D.H.2, which he forced down on the morning of 14 September. It was his second victory that day, he recounted: 'Number 23 was a stubborn opponent. I cut in front of [two aeroplanes] from a flight and went after the second one. The first one ran away. The third was attacked by Leutnant von Richthofen, soon joined by Leutnant [Erwin] Böhme and Leutnant [Hans]

Reimann, but unfortunately it escaped to the Front. At the first attack, my opponent spun down several hundred metres, but then continued on. As I know this trick, I went right after him ... [and] he did not succeed; rather, he crashed near Morval ... A short time later I saw some Englishmen buzzing about north of Puisieux. When I approached, they came after me. As I was sauntering in the air quite harmlessly (that is, I was below them and could do nothing!), I turned away. Since they did not start anything with me, one of the opponents went after another German. But I could not stand that [and proceeded] to make him pay for it. During the dogfight, in addition to puncturing his fuel and oil tanks, I shot him in the right thigh. He landed and was taken prisoner. That was Number 24.'[2]

Below: Manfred von Richthofen gained air combat experience in Fokker biplanes, but achieved success only after Jagdstaffel 2 received Albatros D.II fighters. Wearing riding-breeches and a sweater, he is seen here relaxing in front of a new 'mount' at Lagnicourt airfield with (from left): Oberleutnant Stephan Kirmaier; Leutnant Hans Imelmann; and Leutnant Hans Wortmann. Richthofen's broad grin was well earned, as he noted about his transition to successful airfighter in a letter to his mother on 18 September 1916: 'Recently I flew a temporarily assigned

machine, with which I scarcely got going and could stay at most a short time in aerial combat. Finally, yesterday the appropriate crate arrived for me and, what do you think, while on a test-flight in it I saw a British formation on our side of the lines. I flew there – and shot one down. The crewmen were a British officer and non-commissioned officer [sic]. I was very proud of my test-flight. The downing of the aircraft was, of course, credited to me. The Battle of the Somme is not quite as it seems to you at home. The opponent attacks with enormously superior forces ... [which] have changed the face of mobile warfare. Surely, you know that my friend [Leutnant Hans von] Schweinichen has fallen. I wanted to visit him, as he was right in my area.'[3]

Right: When the *Ehrenbecher* (Cup of Honour) was established to reward combat airmen for shooting down enemy aeroplanes, the first two were presented to Oswald Boelcke and Max Immelmann on Christmas Eve 1915. Boelcke described the scene: 'In the evening we officers exchanged Christmas presents in the officers' mess, where at the same time various awards were distributed. For me there was a very beautiful silver goblet next to other small articles. This goblet, bearing the inscription *"Dem Sieger im Luftkampf"* [To the Victor in Aerial Combat], had been presented to me by the Chief of Field Aviation [Major Hermann von der Lieth-Thomsen]. Immelmann received the same.'[4] Boelcke had scored six victories and Immelmann seven at the time they received their one-litre silver goblets, which were produced at the direction of Kaiser Wilhelm II by Godet, an exclusive goldsmith in Berlin.[5] Later air unit leaders presented goblets to their men – officers and enlisted alike – on

of small, plain silver cups to mark his victories. It was inscribed '1. Vickers 2. 17.9.16' to indicate his first victory, scored over a 'pusher'-type two-seater on 17 September 1916. Some seventeen years later a British journalist visited Richthofen's home in Schweidnitz and described the display seen at the right of this photograph: 'Perhaps the most interesting thing in this room is a glass case filled with little silver cups which a Berlin jeweller made to Manfred's order on confirmation of each victory; these cups do not total 80, because towards the end of the war Germany was running short of silver, but all the same, they make an imposing array; the case also contains a cup won by Richthofen in his cavalry days, as well as numerous gifts to [his mother] Freifrau von Richthofen ... '[6]

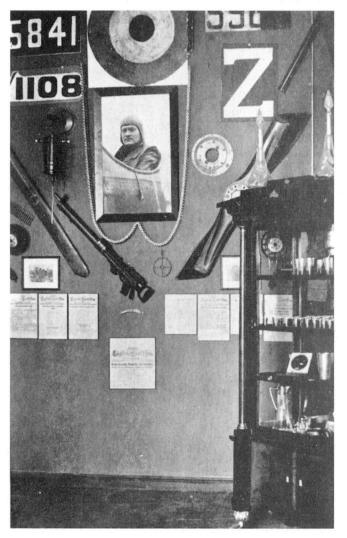

the occasion of their first combat success. Thus in 1916 Boelcke presented an *Ehrenbecher* to Manfred von Richthofen, who, in turn, bestowed similar goblets to men who served under him.

Right: On the evening after Manfred von Richthofen's first confirmed victory, Boelcke had a celebration for the Jasta 2 men who had scored that day. Leutnant Erwin Böhme, who also recorded his first victory, received the Iron Cross 1st Class from Boelcke. Richthofen's old rival, Leutnant der Reserve Hans Reimann, was toasted for his second triumph. It was too soon for Richthofen to receive his *Ehrenbecher*, which Boelcke had to request with proper documentation to verify the award. As if anticipating that some day he would have a great collection of war souvenirs, Richthofen ordered the first of a series

Right: Ever the hunter, Manfred collected combat trophies, as he wrote home: 'On 30 September I shot down my third Englishman. He fell burning. One's heart beats faster when the opponent, whose face one has just seen, rushes into the abyss on fire from 4,000 metres. Down below, there was of course very little remaining of the men or the machine. I took a small insignia as a souvenir. From my second [victory] I kept the machine-gun as a souvenir. It has a bullet of mine in the bolt and is useless.'[7] Another trophy was the swatch of fabric bearing the serial number of Richthofen's fourth victim, B.E.12 6618, which he shot down on 7 October 1916. Here, two ground-crew view the wreckage of that aeroplane. The weekly report of 1. Armee's Staff Officer in Charge of Aviation clearly identified his opponent: 'A British single-seat *Rumpfdoppeldecker* [biplane with a fuselage] was shot down by Leutnant von Richthofen ... at 9.10 a.m. The crewman, Lieutenant Fenwich [*sic*], is dead. The aeroplane was a new type B.E.'[8] Aircraft information and the name of the pilot were recorded with diligence, but less attention was paid to the body of 19-year-old 2/Lt William C. Fenwick, which to this day has no known grave.[9]

Right: Three days later Richthofen claimed to have shot down an F.E.2b 'Vikkers' over the village of Ytres, east of Léchelle. He wanted credit for his fifth victory – three short of the number that he thought would lead to his being awarded the *Orden Pour le Mérite*. He was unpleasantly surprised when credit was awarded to the Feldflieger-Abteilung 22 crew of Offizierstellvertreter (Acting Officer) Fritz Kosmahl, seen here, and his observer, Oberleutnant der Landwehr (First Lieutenant in the Militia) Josef Neubürger, who reported having a prolonged fight with the same RFC two-seater. Richthofen could not disprove their claim because the German two-seater

crew had been closer to the British machine. Richthofen learned from that encounter to stay with his quarry, as he wrote: 'When I approach to within 50 metres of the enemy and draw a bead on him, then [he] must be hit ... I told that to many young men with whom I have flown and have observed. They told me afterwards that they had approached up to ten metres [away from their targets]. I am not exag-

vious to death. Richthofen expressed it best: '... we flew against the enemy under the leadership of The Great Man. One always had the most secure feeling when he was along. There was only one Boelcke.'[11] Richthofen described his idol's last moments on that autumn afternoon: 'Boelcke, some other gentlemen of the Jagdstaffel and I were involved in air combat with Englishmen. Suddenly I saw that Boelcke, while attacking an Englishman, was rammed by one of our gentlemen in the air. Nothing further happened to the other poor gentleman. At first Boelcke descended quite normally. I followed him immediately. [Moments] later, one of the wings broke away and he rushed into the abyss. His skull was crushed on impact, killing him instantly.'[12]

gerating when I say that one could safely add two zeroes to their figures. But that is what these good men miscalculated in the heat of battle ... This kind of people-hunting must really be practised.'[10]

Above: The greatest German practitioner of this form of aerial hunting was Hauptmann Oswald Boelcke. On Saturday, 28 October 1916, Boelcke lay dead near his aircraft in an open field, as would his most successful student, Manfred von Richthofen, 80 weeks and one day later. Boelcke had been so successful in the world's most dangerous profession – front-line combatant – that he seemed to be imper-

Below: Boelcke had accidentally collided with Leutnant Erwin Böhme, who survived and went on to become a significant fighter ace (see Appendix I). Richthofen (arrowed) was accorded the special honour of carrying the pillow bearing his leader's

awards at the funeral service in Cambrai. Later he wrote about Boelcke in terms that would be used to describe Richthofen himself: 'It is characteristic [of Boelcke] that every person who met him imagined that he had been best friends with him ... People whose names he never knew believed that they were especially close to him. It is a peculiar phenomenon that I have observed only with him. He never had a personal enemy. He was equally pleasant to everyone, not more so to some and less so to others. The one person who perhaps stood closest to him was the one who had the ... accident with him.'[13]

Above right: Surprisingly for a prominent air warrior, Oswald Boelcke received only fourteen awards, compared to the 24 decorations ultimately bestowed on Manfred von Richthofen. The black velvet *Orden-skissen* (Cushion with Decorations) which Richthofen carried at the funeral, seen here, displayed Boelcke's *Pour le Mérite* at the top. In the first row from left: Army Pilot's Badge; Iron Cross 2nd Class; Kingdom of Prussia's Knight's Cross of the Royal Order of the House of Hohenzollern with Swords; Prussia's Life-Saving Medal; Duchy of Anhalt's House Order of Albert the Bear Knight's Crosses 1st and 2nd Class with Swords; Duchy of Anhalt's Friedrich Cross; Kingdom of Bavaria's Merit Order 4th Class with Swords; Ottoman Empire's Pilot's Badge. Second row from left: Kingdom of Bulgaria's Bravery Order 2nd Degree; Kingdom of Württemberg's Knight's Cross of the Military Merit Order; Iron Cross 1st Class; Ottoman Empire's Imtiaz Medal in Silver. In his letter of 3 November 1916, Richthofen saw Boelcke's final honours within the perspective of other events: 'During the funeral service I carried the *Ordenskissen*. The ceremony was like that for a reigning prince. In six weeks we have had six dead and one wounded, two men with their nerves shot and twelve aeroplanes lost. Yesterday I shot down my seventh [enemy aeroplane], and

disposed of the sixth shortly before that. Through all these hard times my nerves have not suffered.'[14]

Opposite page, bottom: Despite his prominent role in Boelcke's funeral cortège, Richthofen was still a minor figure in the German Luftstreitkräfte (Air Force), which evolved from the Flying Service on 8 October 1916. But he had a good connection in Leutnant Fritz von Falkenhayn, a friend from their days in the BAO, seen here (left, with sword) leaving St. Joseph's Church in Cambrai after the funeral. Fritz's father, General der Infanterie Erich von Falkenhayn, had been dismissed as Chief of the German General Staff two months earlier, but not before his son had been assigned to the staff of Major Hermann von der Lieth-Thomsen, Chief of Field Aviation (middle, saluting). Thomsen's deputy, Major Wilhelm Siegert (lower right), developed the BAO. Meanwhile, in addition to the honours Boelcke earned in his lifetime, he received a final tribute from Kaiser Wilhelm II, whose telegram to the family proclaimed: 'On this most painful event, I mourn with the German people the death of your hero-son, my bravest and most successful flying-officer. It was with pride that he was regarded by my army and especially the flying service. It will be with pride that after his death they will keep in mind and struggle to emulate his shining example. May God comfort you in your great sorrow.'[15]

Below: Boelcke's death left a gap in the list of living German heroes and Richthofen intended to fill it. On 9 November 1916 he shot down his eighth enemy aeroplane, a British bomber. While Boelcke and Immelmann had received the *Pour le Mérite* after their eighth victories, by this time the criteria for Prussia's highest bravery award had risen and Richthofen gained only more souvenirs and his first encounter with a member of German royalty. Duke Carl Eduard of Saxe–Coburg–Gotha, seen here with his daughter and wearing the uniform that puzzled Richthofen, was near the crash site of his victim when the ambitious combat pilot tore across an open field in pursuit of victory mementoes. Richthofen wrote that after obtaining his trophies he was summoned to meet an unidentified officer wearing a 'general's trousers, a high award at his neck, but ... [with] a relatively youthful face, [and] indefinable epaulettes ... ' That evening Richthofen was invited to a more formal meeting with the 32-year-old head of one of Europe's most prominent royal houses. 'It was known that the British intended to bomb his headquarters ... [and] I had helped keep the assailants away,' Richthofen wrote. 'For that I received the Oval Silver Duke Carl Eduard Bravery Medal.'[16]

Below: The aeroplanes of Richthofen's victims often suffered extensive damage. This rear-view shows an Airco D.H.2 so badly damaged that its type is hard to discern. (See photograph on page 29 for a comparison.) On 22 November 1916 Boelcke's successor, Oberleutnant Stephan Kirmaier, was killed in a fight with D.H.2s of No. 24 Squadron, RFC. The next day Richthofen led Jagdstaffel 2 against that squadron and killed its commanding officer, 26-year-old Major Lanoe G. Hawker, the first fighter pilot to have received Britain's highest award for valour, the Victoria Cross. Richthofen wrote about his 11th victory: 'The circles we made around each other were so tight that I ... peered directly at him in his cockpit and could observe every move-

Rittmeister Manfred Frhr. von Richthofen

ment of his head ... Gradually, this got to be too much for the worthy sportsman and he had to decide whether to land on our side or fly back to his own lines. Of course, he attempted the latter ... [and] now it was the right moment for me. I followed him from 50 down to 30 metres altitude, firing steadily ... [Then] with a shot in the head, the opponent crashed about 50 metres behind our lines. His machine-gun was rammed into the earth and [after it was recovered] now it graces the entrance over the door to my home.'[17]

Above: After Kirmaier's death, Richthofen became the *de facto* leader of Jagdstaffel 2. Formal command passed to a seasoned pilot and unit leader, Oberleutnant Franz Josef Walz, on 29 November 1916, but Richthofen continued to lead the Staffel in combat success. His efforts were recognised in January 1917,

when he received command of his own unit and then the coveted medal so prominent in this postcard photograph. 'Boelcke and Immelmann had received the *Pour le Mérite* after their eighth victories,' he wrote. 'I had doubled that [score]. What would happen now? I was very excited. It had been rumoured that I would receive a Jagdstaffel. Then [on 10 January] a telegram came, reading: "Leutnant von Richthofen appointed to be leader of Jagdstaffel 11." I must say, I was annoyed. I had become so well acquainted with my comrades in Jagdstaffel Boelcke. Now to have to settle in all over again was irksome. Two days later – we were sitting together cheerfully at Jagdstaffel Boelcke and celebrating my leaving – a telegram from Headquarters came saying that His Majesty [the Kaiser] had the pleasure of awarding me the *Pour le Mérite*. Of course there was great joy. It was a salve to my bruised feelings.'[18]

Above: Richthofen's challenge was to turn Jagdstaffel 11 into a first-rate fighter unit. The Staffel had been established on 28 September 1916, but, as a consequence of poor training and lacklustre leadership, had operated for three months without logging a combat success. Based at La Brayelle, north-west of Douai, Jasta 11 had an undeveloped resource in the cadre of eager young hawks seen here cavalierly smoking cigarettes in front of an outmoded Albatros D.I (beginning with second from left): Leutnant Konstantin Krefft, a pilot with two early combat units who became the Staffel's skilled Technical Officer; Oberleutnant Hans Helmut von Boddien, a pilot from Feldflieger-Abteilung 18 who was destined to join Jasta 11; Leutnant Kurt Wolff, a former Kampfgeschwader pilot who ultimately shot down 33 enemy aeroplanes; Leutnant der Reserve Kurt Küppers, a pre-war pilot who flew on the Eastern

Front before joining Jasta 6 when it was under Richthofen's command; and Leutnant Carl Allmenröder, a Richthofen protégé who became a leading fighter pilot. See Appendix I for more about Allmenröder, Krefft and Wolff. Flying the newer and improved Albatros D.III, Richthofen scored Jasta 11's first – and his own 17th – victory on 23 January 1917, his first day in command.

Above right: The image of the 'Red Baron' was created when Richthofen had his Albatros D.III painted almost entirely red. Even the iron cross national insignia was given a red 'wash' which had to be enhanced in this photograph. 'For whatever reasons, one fine day I hit upon the idea of having my crate painted glaring red. The result was that absolutely everyone knew of my red bird. Also, my opponents seemed to be not completely unaware' of this radical departure in markings, he wrote. To prove the point, Richthofen recounted his 24 January meeting with the crew of the 18th enemy aircraft he brought down, Captain Oscar Greig and Second-Lieutenant John E. MacLenan of No. 25 Squadron: 'They were the first Englishmen I had brought down alive. For that reason I especially enjoyed talking to them. Among other things, I asked them whether they had ever seen my machine in the air before. "Oh yes," one of them said. "I know it quite well. We call it *le petit rouge* [the little red one]."'[19] Richthofen did not mention that he had had a forced landing of his own when MacLenan's machine-gun fire caused one of the Albatros' lower wings to crack.

Right: With his red Albatros D.III temporarily out of service, following his fight with Greig and

MacLenan, Richthofen had to fly a Halberstadt D.II similar to the one seen here. His encounter with the British two-seat reconnaissance aeroplane also cost the German ace a bit of dignity, according to him: 'At about 500 metres' altitude a malfunction in my machine during a normal glide likewise forced me to land without being able to make another turn. Now something quite comical occurred. My enemy landed smoothly in his burning machine, while I, the victor, turned over ... on the barbed wire of the trenches of one of our reserve emplacements ... Then [during the interview with one of the captured crewmen] came what was in my view a typically British mean trick. He asked me why I had acted so carelessly in landing. The reason was that I could not do anything else. Then the scoundrel said that in the final 300 metres he had tried to fire at me, but that he had a

his own propeller. He stopped firing, pulled away and returned to base with the splintered propeller seen here. Schäfer's aeroplane was repaired, after which, he recounted: 'On the 4th [of March] things were much better. Our ... 'Swarm' was made ready; Richthofen wanted to go with us, but had to stay home because of a small defect [in his aeroplane]. So I led the way. We had scarcely arrived at the Front when a British formation appeared, flying low near Loos. We attacked from over Lens; at the same time three Germans from the Böelcke Staffel attacked them. My first opponent eluded me in a steep dive. Before I could follow him I saw Allmenröder being pressed hard by two Englishmen and I gave him some breathing room. As I did, a "Vickers" single-seater got in behind me. I made a half-loop and went into a spin; two comrades who saw it thought I had been shot down, as did the "Vickers" pilot, who then left me alone. I squeezed out of that scrape in such a way that I had a measured look at things and then very calmly went after a Sopwith two-seater. After I fired 100 shots it began to burn, then side-slipped down, fell end over end and fluttered earthwards in a burning heap, whereupon I could not help letting out a loud Hurrah.'[22]

gun-jamb [sic]. I had given him the gift of his life – he took it and subsequently repaid me with an insidious personal attack. Since then I have not been able to speak with any of my opponents, for obvious reasons.'[20] A week and a day later, Richthofen flew the Halberstadt and shot down another two-seater and wounded its crew members so badly that they died shortly afterwards.[21]

Above: Leutnant Karl-Emil Schäfer was flying a new Albatros D.III when he opened fire on his intended first victim with Jagdstaffel 11 on 3 March 1917. The synchronisation gear malfunctioned and he shot into

Below: Flying an F.E.8 single-seat 'pusher' like this captured example from the same unit, Second-Lieutenant Henry C. Todd of No. 40 Squadron RFC was the first British pilot to shoot down Manfred von Richthofen. On the morning of 9 March 1917 German anti-aircraft guns fired at Todd and eight other F.E.8s over Oppy. Todd reported: 'Hostile A.A. suddenly ceased and a formation of eight or more H.A. [hostile aircraft] ... dived down from above the clouds. [My] F.E.8 dived on one H.A. and fired a drum at close range, driving H.A. down to 1,000 ft. H.A. went down appar-

ently out of control, emitting considerable smoke or fuel ...'[23] From Richthofen's account, he was concentrating on another F.E.8 and did not see Todd behind him in the classic 'kill' position: 'Now I am 50 metres away, a few good shots now and then success is inevitable. So I thought. But all of a sudden there is a big bang; I have barely got off ten shots when again there is a smack on my machine. It is clear ... my machine has been [hit, although] I personally have not. At the same moment it stinks something terrible of fuel, also the engine slows down. The Englishman notices it, for now he shoots even more ... I go straight down. Instinctively, I have switched off the engine ... If the fuel tank is punctured and the stuff squirts around my legs, the danger of fire is indeed great ... I am leaving behind me a trail of white mist. I know it very well from [having seen it in] adversaries. It happens just before an explosion.'[24] Richthofen's luck held and he managed to glide into a flat meadow. He caught a ride back to La Brayelle and an hour later was back in the air, successfully attacking his 25th victim.

Right: Just as Boelcke had once attracted the best airfighters, Richthofen's growing reputation motivated pilots in other units to apply for transfer to Jagdstaffel 11. A new pilot who joined the unit on 10 March 1917 was Leutnant Lothar Freiherr von Richthofen (second from left), the younger brother of Manfred (right). He is seen here with (from left) future aces Leutnant der Reserve Hans Weiss and Leutnant Eberhard Mohnike, as well as Hauptmann Wilhelm Haehnelt, Officer in Charge of Aviation for 2. Armee during the March 1918 offensive. Lothar quickly proved that his transfer from Kampfgesch-

wader 4 was based on merit, as Manfred observed: 'He was a ... cautious flyer who did not think about looping and similar tricks, but, rather, was satisfied when he took off and landed properly. Two weeks later I took him with me for the first time against the enemy and had him fly close behind me to just watch things. After the third flight I saw him pull away from me suddenly and dive on an Englishman and bring him down. My heart leapt with joy as I watched this ... Four weeks later my brother had already shot down his 20th Englishman. Surely it must be unique in all of aviation for a pilot to shoot down his first opponent two weeks after passing his third examination and four weeks after that [to have bagged] the first 20.'[25]

Right: After structural problems with the Albatros D.III fighters had been resolved – at least temporarily – Manfred von Richthofen resumed flying his all-red aeroplane. His subordinates also had their machines over-painted mostly in red, with slight variations, such as Leutnant Carl Allmenröder's Albatros, with its distinctive white nose, seen here. Lothar von

Richthofen explained that he and his comrades asked to follow Manfred's example 'so that he would not be so especially conspicuous ... [and because] we had proven ourselves to be worthy of the red colour by our many aerial victories. The red colour signified a certain insolence ... It attracted attention. Consequently, one had to really perform. Proudly we finally looked at our red birds. My brother's crate was glaring red. Each of the rest of us had some additional markings in other colours. As we could not see one another's faces in the air, we chose these colours as recognition symbols. Schäfer, for example, had his elevator, rudder and most of the back part of the fuselage [painted] black; Allmenröder used white [on the nose and spinner], Wolff used green and I had yellow. Each one of us was different. In the air and from the ground, as well as from the enemy's view, we all looked to be red, as only small other parts were painted in another colour.'[26]

Right: Manfred von Richthofen's first Albatros D.III was passed down to Lothar, seen here receiving advice from Carl Allmenröder. Some sources indicate that the aircraft was mahogany-coloured with a red band, barely visible here, between the cockpit and national marking.[27] Lothar regarded the aeroplane and a pair of Manfred's old flying-gloves as talismanic, keeping him from harm and aiding his early success. 'As luck would have it, I shot down my first ten Englishmen armed with these gloves and this machine,' Lothar wrote. 'After these ten victories our old crate, which had a red band around the fuselage, was so riddled with bullet holes that the trusty steed had to be transported home. Manfred was also attached to his famous red bird ... One fine day Schäfer wanted to fly the red bird. When he returned from the flight, he declared in horror that simply flying this rattle-trap was

mortally dangerous. He asserted that it creaked in every joint. In Manfred's devotion to his machine he ignored completely his own [prospects for] advanced age.'[28]

Below: As a fighter pilot, Manfred had found his calling. The one-time lacklustre cadet had developed into an effective combat leader and gained appropriate recognition. He was even promoted ahead of the class of officers with whom he had been commissioned[29] and had the special pleasure of watching his brother's career advance. On 26 March Manfred, here wearing the newly earned rank insignia of an Oberleutnant (First Lieutenant), wrote home:

'Yesterday I shot down [my] 31st, the day before the 30th. Three days ago I was promoted to Oberleutnant by order of the Royal Cabinet of Ministers. I have therefore gained a good half-year's seniority. My Staffel is doing well ... Yesterday, Lothar had his first aerial combat. He was very satisfied because he hit his adversary. We say that [the victim] "stank", because he left behind him a ribbon of black smoke. Of course, he did not crash, as that would have been too much luck for the first time. Lothar is very conscientious and he will do well.'[30] Manfred did not remain an Oberleutnant for long; fifteen days later he was promoted to Rittmeister (Cavalry Captain) – a considerable achievement for a 24-year-old officer.

Opposite page, top: In happier times, Manfred von Richthofen (with walking-stick) enjoys a visit to the two-seat reconnaissance unit Flieger-Abteilung (A)

258 and its commanding officer, Prince Friedrich Karl of Prussia (third from right). Manfred and the Prince had been friends since their cadet days; both had begun their army careers in hussar regiments and then joined the aviation service. Prince Friedrich Karl was a cousin of Kaiser Wilhelm II and, true to the Hohenzollern warrior tradition, was in the fore-front of military activity. Flying two-seaters was too calm for him and he also flew fighter patrols with Jagdstaffel 2 in an Albatros D.I (background, right) decorated with the hussars' death's head insignia.

Left: Prince Friedrich Karl of Prussia, seen here in a popular postcard photograph, was forced down behind British lines on 21 March 1917 to become the fourth victim of Lieutenant Charles E. M. Pickthorne. According to the official British report: 'Lieut. Pickthorne, No. 32 Squadron, got on the tail of an Albatros Scout, which he forced to land near Vaulx-Vraucourt, the pilot (Prince Frederick Charles of Prussia) being wounded.'[31]

Right: The captured Albatros D.I flown by Prince Friedrich Karl was hauled away as a worthy prize, and the pilot was sent to a prisoner of war camp at St-Etienne, near Rouen. A brave, resourceful soldier, the Prince sought to escape from captivity on 6 April 1917, his 24th birthday, and was fatally wounded in the attempt.[32]

Below: The pilot of this captured SPAD S.7 of No. 19 Squadron, RFC, was lucky. When his aeroplane developed engine trouble over the German lines on 18 May 1917, Second-Lieutenant J. D. V. Holmes landed unharmed and was taken prisoner. The engine was repaired and German insignia were applied to the aeroplane so that it could be test flown to evaluate its capabilities. Two months earlier, on 24 March, Holmes' squadron mate, Lieutenant Richard P. Baker, was trying to fix his malfunctioning engine when an all-red Albatros D.III appeared above him. Baker tried to get back to his own side of the lines, but to no avail, as Manfred von Richthofen noted in describing his 30th combat triumph: 'Two new single-seaters ... were flying nearby. They were extremely fast and handy. I attacked one of them and ascertained that my machine was the better one. After a long fight I managed to hit the adversary's fuel tank. The propeller stopped. The aeroplane had to go down. As the fight had taken place above [German] trenches, my adversary tried to escape, but I managed to force him to land behind our lines near Givenchy. The aeroplane turned over in a shellhole, upside down, and was taken by our troops.'[33] The SPAD's Canadian pilot was wounded in the knee and, after receiving medical treatment, spent the remainder of the war in various prison camps.

Below: April 1917 was the best month of Manfred von Richthofen's combat career. He shot down his 32nd victim on the 2nd, and on the 29th he achieved victories 49 to 52 within the space of eight hours. Sitting in the cockpit of his all-red Albatros D.III, he is seen here with Jagdstaffel 11 comrades; their April scores are shown in brackets after their names. From left standing: Leutnant Carl Allmenröder (6 to 9); Leutnant der Reserve Hans Hintsch; Vizefeldwebel Sebastian Festner (3 to 12, killed on 23 April); Leutnant Karl-Emil Schäfer (9 to 23); Leutnant Kurt Wolff (6 to 27); Leutnant Georg Simon; Leutnant der Reserve Otto Brauneck. From left seated: Leut-nant Karl Esser; Leutnant der Reserve Konstantin Krefft; Leutnant Lothar von Richthofen (2 to 16). Wind and rain seemed to offer little obstacle to Manfred's prowess, as he noted in describing his morning battle on 2 April: 'Suddenly, one of the cheeky fellows jumped me, trying to force me down. Calmly, I let him come down and then we began a merry dance. Sometimes my opponent flew on his back, sometimes this way, sometimes that. It was a two-seat combat aeroplane. I was superior to him and soon realised that he could not escape me ... Therefore, whoever shot better, remained the calmest and had the best perspective at the moment

of danger would win. It did not take long. I squeezed under him and fired ... When only a few metres above the ground, he suddenly levelled off and flew straight ahead ... I could not let up now ... He crashed at full speed into a block of houses, and there was not much left.'[1]

Below: Richthofen scored a second victory on 2 April, while flying with Jagdstaffel 2's Leutnant Werner Voss, who received the *Pour le Mérite* six days later, as seen here. 'The day before Voss had finished off his 23rd [victim],' Richthofen wrote. 'Therefore, he ranked next to me and was then my most vigorous competitor. As he flew home I accompanied him for a short distance. The weather had really become very bad ... [and] Voss, who did not know the area, began to get uncomfortable. Over Arras I met my brother, who ... had become

lost from his group. He joined up with us. He knew that it was me in the red bird. Then we saw an enemy flight approaching. Immediately "Number Thirty-three" flashed into my head. Even though there were nine Englishmen and over their own territory, they preferred to avoid combat ... But we caught up with them ... I was closest to the enemy and attacked the one farthest back. To my great delight, he also wanted to engage me in combat ... He knew what it was all about and, especially, the guy was a good shot ... [But then] my opponent noticed that the situation was not as simple as he thought and disappeared in a steep dive into a cloud. That was almost his salvation. I dived after him, came out below and ... by some miracle, I was sitting behind him. I fired and fired ... Then, finally, I hit him. I noticed the white vapour of fuel that remained behind his machine. He had to land, for his engine had quit.'[2]

Left: Werner Voss was almost five years younger than Richthofen, but was just as determined an airfighter. He was relatively inactive during 'Bloody April' – so called by the British because of the very high level of air casualties sustained – and shot down only two aeroplanes that month. But he displayed the seasoned fighter pilot's necessary emotional hardness following his involvement in Richthofen's 33rd victory. Richthofen presents a hint of sportsmanlike behaviour in contrast to Voss' colder view of aerial combat: '[The Englishman] must have recognised that he was all done. If he had continued to fire [at me], I could have shot him dead immediately, for in the meantime we had come down to only 300 metres. But the fellow defended himself, just as did the one from that morning, until he landed. After his landing I flew over him again at ten metres' altitude to determine whether or not I had shot him dead. And what did the fellow do? He took his machine-gun and shot up my whole machine. Voss said to me later that, if it had happened to him, he would have flown back and shot [the Englishman] dead on the ground. In fact, I should have done it, for he had not really surrendered. He was, indeed, one of the few lucky ones who remained alive.'[3]

Below: The RFC's Bristol F.2A was intended to counter the German aeronautical improvements of late 1916 and early 1917. Fast and agile, it offered a wide field of vision for the pilot's forward-firing gun and less restriction of the observer/gunner's gun as a consequence of the low rudder design. The first F.2A unit to go into battle was No. 48 Squadron, to which this machine from the first production batch[4] was assigned. Unfortunately for their crews, early F.2As had operating problems and the first offensive patrol, on 5 April 1917, was a disaster for the Royal Flying Corps and a bonanza for Jagdstaffel 11. Richthofen reported: 'I attacked with four aeroplanes of my Staffel. I personally singled out the last machine, which I forced to land after a short fight near Lewarde. The crew burned their machine. It was a new type of aeroplane, which we had not yet seen; it appears to be quick and rather [manoeuvrable]. A powerful engine, V-shaped [with] 12 cylinders; its manufacturer could not be determined. The [Albatros] D.III is undoubtedly superior, both in speed and in climbing ability. Of the enemy flight, which consisted of six aeroplanes, four were forced to land on our side by my Staffel.'[5]

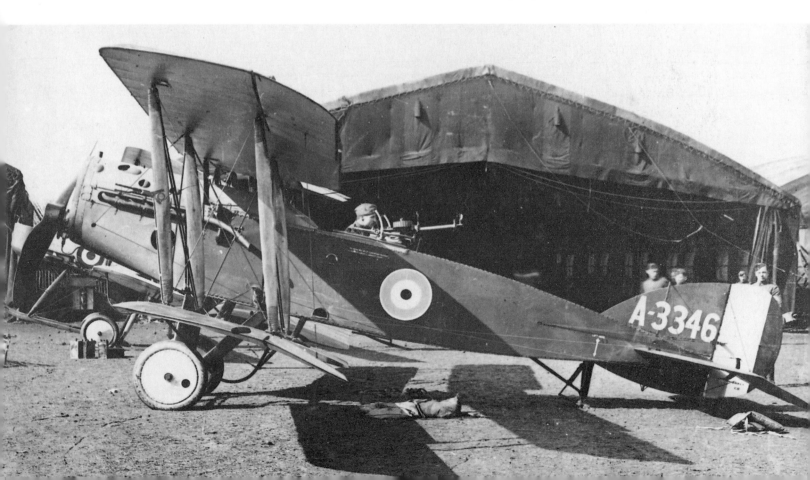

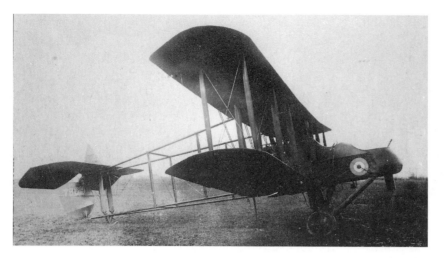

he had shot down nine of them to date. It had been a formidable opponent; the observer in the front cockpit had a forward-firing machine-gun and another gun for firing aft. Despite this and further night-bombing raids by F.E.2s, Richthofen was contemptuous of them: 'It was quite an old crate. We recognised the type precisely ... I find that, in general, bombing at night has significance only on morale. If one fills his pants [because of it], then it is very embarrassing for him, but not for the others.'[8]

Above: While Jagdstaffel 11 celebrated its recent successes, that evening the Royal Flying Corps struck back. Eighteen F.E.2b bombers – including No. 7669, seen here, which was forced down in German territory two nights later[6] – made a night raid on German airfields near Douai. According to the RFC report: 'On the night of the 5th, 6th [April], Douai Aerodrome was attacked twice by machines of No. 100 Squadron. Four hangars were completely destroyed and other damage was done. On the day of the 6th, 13 phosphorous and 97 20lb. bombs were dropped on various targets.'[7] Richthofen knew his adversary, as his first confirmed victory had been an F.E.2 and

Below: This photograph from the Richthofen Museum shows how completely an aeroplane identical to the ace's 37th victim could be destroyed in a crash. Only the sesquiplane bottom wing (right foreground), the tail (left) and the distinctive cowling remained to indicate that it had been a French-built Nieuport 17. Of the fight on 7 April 1917, Richthofen reported: 'Together with four of my gentlemen I attacked an enemy flight of six Nieuport machines, south of Arras and behind enemy lines. The aeroplane I singled out tried to escape six times by various manoeuvres. When he was doing this for the seventh time, I managed to

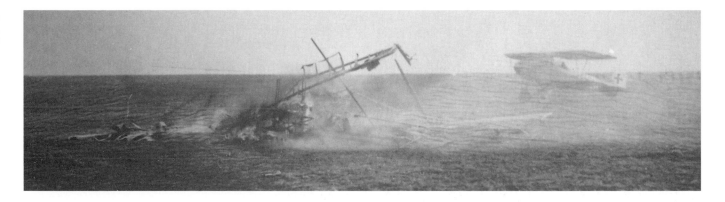

hit him, whereupon his engine began to smoke and burn, and the aeroplane itself went down head first, spinning and spinning. At first I thought it might be another manoeuvre, but then I saw the aeroplane dive, without catching itself, into the ground near Mercatel.'[9] Jagdstaffel 11 claimed three Nieuports of No. 60 Squadron, all shot down at about 1745 hours; but the RFC reported losing only two aeroplanes in that fight. That all three victory claims were credited – one each to Richthofen, Wolff and Schäfer – is a reflection on the confusing nature of aerial combat in general; the many tenuous claims confirmed and firmer claims disallowed were common to both sides. More than eight decades later, aviation historians continue to debate various claims and credits.

Above: The month's first break in the weather came on Easter Sunday, 8 April 1917, when Jagdstaffel 11 was credited with shooting down five British aeroplanes. All of them fell in German-held territory, making scenes such as this common: a smouldering victim in the foreground with the victor taxiing past it. Leutnant Karl-Emil Schäfer described a scene that may have occurred on Holy Saturday evening to set the stage for the following day's successes: 'Finally the barometer began to climb, the "weather frog" [meteorologist] predicted beautiful weather ... [which] let us hope for the best for the next day. We went to bed early to be well-rested and in saying our good-nights [added]: "Tomorrow it must rain the blood of British pilots!" That sounds very bloodthirsty, but in reality was not meant to be so wicked, for we would have preferred it when some poor wretch landed safely

near us than when he simply came down in tatters or as a pitiful piece of coal and ash.'[10]

Below: Manfred's Easter morning victim was a 1½-Strutter piloted by 20-year-old Second Lieutenant John S. Heagerty, seen here after the war in his Royal Air Force uniform. Heagerty and his observer, Lieutenant Leonard Heath Cantle, a year older, were part of a flight patrolling the lines from Arras to Lens. About midway, trouble descended upon them, as

Richthofen's combat report states: 'With three of my aeroplanes I attacked three Sopwiths over Farbus. The aeroplane I singled out soon made a right-hand turn downwards. The observer ceased shooting. I followed the adversary to the ground, where it smashed to pieces.' Heagerty recalled: 'The German scouts ... seemed to drop down from all directions, pumping lead as they came. Cantle was working the aft Lewis [machine-gun] and I heard him let out a good blast at someone in back of us ... I kicked over the rudder just in time to see the red 'plane passing below. We swerved at the same time, and 'round and 'round we went, each trying to get on the other's tail ... Cantle's gun was rattling away, when suddenly he ceased firing and, at the same time, the pressure on [my] joystick was suddenly released. It was useless. My controls ... must have gone in the same burst that killed Cantle.'[11] The aeroplane crashed and Heagerty was badly injured, but survived the war. Cantle's body was left alongside the wreckage and was buried eight days later when British XIII Corps forces captured the area.[12]

Below: Oberst (Colonel) Hermann von der Lieth-Thomsen, Air Chief of Staff (left), and Generalleutnant (Lieutenant-General) Ernst von Hoeppner, Commanding General of the Air Force, posing with Richthofen at Supreme High Command Headquarters in Bad Kreuznach, Germany, several weeks after they received the *Orden Pour le Mérite*. On Easter Sunday 1917, Kaiser Wilhelm II authorised the awards in recognition of their leadership and successful re-organisation of the Luftstreitkräfte (Air Force).[13] In 1910 Thomsen and future General Erich von Ludendorff became their country's first general staff officers to fly and evaluate the value of the aeroplane for reconnaissance.[14] When the former German Fliegertrupppe (Flying Service) began to lose momentum in the late summer of 1916, von Hoeppner, a former cavalry officer, was brought in and successfully re-shaped the organisation.

Opposite page top: Jagdstaffel 11 on the flight-line, seen here, became a news event when *Kölnische Zeitung* correspondent Prof. Dr. Georg Wegener arrived at La Brayelle airfield on 11 April. His effusive article about such colourful combat aeroplanes as Leutnant Carl Allmenröder's white-nosed Albatros (right) observed: 'From a distance they looked like iridescent giant insects, like a swarm of gaily coloured butterflies with their wings spread out, sunning themselves on the ground. The principle of looking as much as

Oberstleutnant Thomsen
Chef des Generalstabes
der Luftstreitkräfte

Rittmeister
Freiherr v. Richthofen
unser erfolgreichster Flieger

Generalleutnant von Hoeppner

possible like the colour of the sky was entirely abandoned ... For this reason every pilot has his personal machine, in which he always flies and to which he is so closely attached as if with a living creature, giving it a special marking that enables his comrades to keep him in sight during combat and to know at all times who controls the machine. One machine has white or red or some other coloured stripes, another carries them diagonally or longitudinally, etc. From Richthofen's eyes shine the pride of the warrior knight, whose shield and helmet ornament are known and feared by the opponent. "I make sure that my flight sees me wherever I am," [he said].[15] Wegener viewed one of Jasta 11's most successful combats through the long telescope seen at the right.

Below: Unlucky Friday the 13th applied more to the Royal Flying Corps in April 1917 than to Jagdstaffel 11, as shown by these two pages from the weekly report of 6. Armee's Officer in Charge of Aviation.

---

am 8.4.17:
7.00 nachm. 1 F.E.-Zweisitzer bei La Bassée (diesseits) durch M.G. abgeschossen.
am 9.4.17:
7.10 nachm. 1 B.E.-Zweisitzer bei Aix-Noulette (diesseits) dch.Lt.Schaefer, J.St.11 (als 14.)
am 11.4.17:
9.05 vorm. 1 Bristol-D.D. bei Pampoux (jenseits) durch Vzfw.Festner, J.St.11 (als 9.)
9.10 vorm. 1 B.E.-D.D. bei Pampoux (jenseits) durch Lt.Schaefer, J.St.11 (als 15.)
9.10 vorm. 1 B.E.-D.D. bei Mouville Fe (diesseits) durch Lt.Wolff,J.St.11 (als 9.)
9.10 vorm. 1 B.E.-D.D. bei Mouville Fe (diesseits) durch Lt.Frhr.v.Richthofen, J.St.11 (als ?.)
9.25 vorm. 1 B.E.-D.D. bei Willerval (diesseits) durch Rittm.Frhr:v.Richthofen,J.St.11 (als 40.)
10.20 vorm. 1 fdl.Flgz. bei Vitry (diesseits) durch Lt.Klein,J.St.4 (als 4.)
10.50 vorm. 1 fdl.Flgs. bei Roeux (jenseits) durch Lt.Klein, J.St.4 (als 5.)
12.50 nachm. 1 Sopwith-Zweisitzer oestl.Arras (jenseits) durch Schaefer, J.St.11 (als 16.)
12.50 nachm. 1 Sopwith-Zweisitzer bei Pampoux (jenseits) durch Lt.Frhr.von Richthofen, J.St.11 (als43.)
am 12.4.17:
10.35 vorm.1 Sopwith-Zweisitzer bei Bourlon (diesseits) durch Hptm.von Osterroth, Fuehrer von J.St.12 (als 8.)
10.35 vorm. 1 F.E.-D.D. bei Dury (diesseits) durch Vzfw.Schorisch, J.St.12
10.40 vorm. 1 F.E.-D.D. bei Bourlon (diesseits) durch Lt.Schulthe, J.St.12 (als 14.)
am 13.4.17:
8.56 vorm. 1 F.E.-D.D. bei Vitry (diesseits) durch Rittm.Frhr.von Richthofen,J.St.11 (als 41.)
8.56 vorm. 1 Bristol-D.D. bei Vitry (diesseits) durch Lt.Wolff, J.St. 11 (als 10.)
8.56 vorm. 1 Bristol-D.D. nordwestl.Vitry (diesseits) durch Lt.Klein, J.St.4 (als 6.)
8.31 vorm. 1 F.E.-D.D. s.Dury (diesseits) durch Vzf.Festner, J.St.11 (als 9.)
8.55 vorm. 2 B.E.-D.D. bei Biache u.Pelves (diesseits) durch Lt.Frhr.von Richthofen,J.St.11 (als4.u.5.)
12.35 nachm. 1 F.E.-D.D. suedl.Bailleul (jenseits) durch Lt.Wolff,J.St. 11 (als 11.)
12.45 nachm. 1 F.E.-D.D. westl.Monchy (jenseits) durch Rittm.Frhr.von Richthofen, J.St.11 (als 42.)
3.20 N. 1 fdl.Flgs. bei Quiery la Motte (diess.) durch Flak.
4.30 N. je 1 Nieuport-Einsitzer bei Monchy (jens.) durch Lt.Wolff,J.St. 11 (als 12.) u. Lt.Schaefer, J.St.11 (als 17.)
6.40 N. 1 B.E.-D.D. bei Point du jour (jenseits) durch Lt.Schaefer, J.St.11 (als 18.)
6.52 N. 1 F.E.-Zweisitzer bei Rouvroy (diesseits) durch Lt.Wolff, J.St.11 (als 13.)
7.10 N. 1 F.E.-D.D. bei Vimy (diess) durch Lt.Klein, J.St.4 (als 7.)
7.15 N. 1 B.E.-D.D. bei La Bassée (diess.) durch Lt.Bauer, J.St.3 .

---

am 13.4.17:
7.30 N. 1 B.E.-D;D. bei Harnes (diess.) durch Lt. Schaefer, J.St.11 (als19.)
7.30 N. 1 F.E.-D.D. oestl.Harnes (diess.) durch Vzfw.Festner, J.St.11 (als 10.)
7.30 N. 1 F.E.-D.D. bei Henin-Lietard (diess.)durch Rittm.Frhr.v.Richthofen,J.St.11 (als 43.)

Am 13.4.17 9.00 V. wurde 1 fdl.Geschwader von 6 Flgs. westl. Douai durch J.St.11 gaenzlich aufgerieben.
Waehrend der Berichtwoche wurden also im ganzen abgeschossen:
46 fdl. Flugzeuge
davon innerhalb unserer Linien: 30.

Ausserdem wurde, wie schon im vorigen Bericht erwaehnt, 1 fdl. Fesselballon w.Arras am 7.4.17 5.00 N. dch.Lt.Klein, J.St.4, abgeschossen.

11.) Eigene Verluste:

Am 7.4.17 Ru:0 I 2605/16 Fuehrer Gefr.Schoop, Sch.St.7, Beob. Lt.Hupe,Fl.A,(A) 233 vom Frontflug nicht zurueckgekehrt.
Am 8.4.17 Lt.Frankl,Ritter des Ordens Pour le Merite, J.St.4, im Luftkampf ueber Vitry gefallen.
Am 9.4.17 Lt.Schroeder, Fl.A.(A) 202 im Luftkampf verwundet.
Am 12.4.17 Lt.Schulthe, J.St.12, rammte im Luftkampf ueber Groisilles 1 engl.Flgs. u.stuerzte mit diesem toetlich ab.
Am 13.4.17 U.O.Binder, Sch.St.24, im Luftkampf schwer verwundet.

12.) Besonderes:

Bei feindl.Bombenangriff auf Flugplatz Douai brannte 1 Zelt (Sch.St.7) vollstaendig nieder.
2 fdl.Fesselballone von Arras ueber die Linie getrieben.
Mehrere Funker durch Artillerie-Feuer getoetet.
Nach Abwurfmeldung engl.Flieger befindet sich Lt.Flink verwundet in engl.Gefangenschaft.

Srg.

On that day the Richthofen brothers and their comrades dominated the Arras sector and outperformed all other Jastas, as well as their adversaries. Relatively modest success on Wednesday, 11 April – seven out of nine scored on 6. Armee's front – was followed two days later by the best day in Jasta 11's history. Of the sixteen victories confirmed that day for the sector, twelve were credited to Jasta 11 after fighting that had lasted from morning until evening. Rittmeister Manfred von Richthofen led the day's scoring with his 41st victory at 0856 hours. He shot down his 42nd opponent at 1145 and concluded the day's achievements with his 43rd victory at 1930 hours. Times and places for all of the day's scoring – including Lothar von Richthofen's 4th and 5th, and Kurt Wolff's 10th to 13th – were clearly identified and correspond with known RFC losses. Item No. 11 on the second page of this report verifies that Jasta 11's stunning performance for the week was not offset by losses. A significant 6. Armee casualty was reported for 8 April, however, when Leutnant Wilhelm Frankl, leader of Jasta 4 and the only Jewish recipient of the *Orden Pour le Mérite*, fell in combat over Vitry.

Above: Still smouldering, one of four new R.E.8 two-seaters brought down by Jagdstaffel 11 on the morning of 13 April is examined by German troops in the area. A flight of six R.E.8s from No. 59 Squadron was wiped out while heading for a photo-reconnaissance mission over Etaing, south-east of Jasta 11's airfield. Leutnant Kurt Wolff destroyed one of them, Lothar von Richthofen was credited with two and Manfred von Richthofen shot down one, which was the first of his three 'kills' that day. Visiting journalist Wegener witnessed the apparent ease with which the Jasta 11 pilots had fought and reported the sobering aftermath: 'No one was injured. It all looked like it could have been a successful sporting event. But Richthofen's machine showed how little it was really like that. An enemy machine-gun burst hit [his] lower left wing and the fabric for about a metre and a half looked as if it had been slashed open by the swipe of a big knife. And on the outer wooden covering close to the pilot's seat ran a second scar showing that another shot had come close to taking his life.'[16]

Right: A crashed British aeroplane (arrowed) lay neglected in the shell-pocked desert between the lines near Bullecourt, north-east of Bapaume, when it was photographed by a German reconnaissance aeroplane on 14 April. It is a tribute to Royal Flying Corps and Royal Naval Air Service crews that in a 4-

week period of such heavy losses – 912 pilots and observers in 50 squadrons, about one-third of British air strength on the Western Front[17] – they persevered and, indeed, recovered their ability to bring the war to their adversaries. The value of each airman, irrespective of nationality, was aptly phrased by Richthofen: 'Airfighting in this world war is the last vestige of knightly individual combat. A hundred years ago the leader of an army stood on his hilltop command post and from there directed the battle and, when it went badly, led the attack himself. Now, the army leader sits at the telephone for hours, has the situation map under his nose and storms against bits of paper that represent nests of Englishmen. It is different in the air. There one finds no General Staff officer to lead the attack against an enemy formation

... One just flies toward the British formation, then there is a battle and it ends in individual combat. I do not pin down the enemy formation with my machine-gun; rather, I seek out a single opponent. Then it is a matter of: you or me!'[18]

Above: Old comrades were reunited when Richthofen visited his former *Brieftauben-Abteilung* pilot, Hauptmann Paul Henning von Osterroht, on 15 April 1917. Osterroht, a career army officer and pre-war aviator, was then commanding Jagdstaffel 12. Richthofen recalled his former superior as an intrepid pilot: 'Once I flew with Osterroht, who had a somewhat smaller aeroplane than our old [AEG G.II]. About five kilometres behind [French lines] we encountered a Farman two-seater. Osterroht

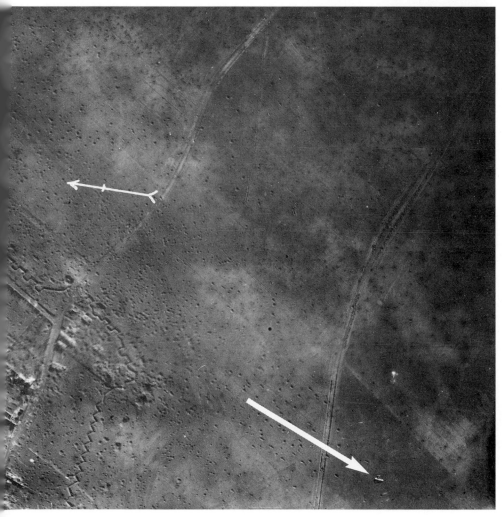

calmly brought us near him and for the first time I saw an adversary in the air right next to us. Osterroht flew very skilfully [and] so close that I could easily bring him under fire. The adversary had not noticed us at all, for it was not until the first time my gun jambed that he began to return fire. After I fired my first drum of a hundred rounds, I could not believe my eyes; all of a sudden the adversary went down in a curious spiral ... and then dropped into a big bomb crater; we saw it standing on its nose, tail high in the air. On a map I determined that it was five kilometres behind the lines then in effect. At that time, however, aeroplanes shot down on the other side did not count; otherwise I would have one more on my victory list.'[19] At the time when this photograph was taken Richthofen had 44 victories to his credit and Osterroht five.

Below: On 16 April, because of increasing British attacks on La Brayelle airfield, Jagdstaffel 11 was moved to Roucourt, south-east of Douai, where the officers were billeted in an elegant château. Here, Major Albrecht Freiherr von Richthofen (third from right) is seen during a visit to the new quarters. He was warmly welcomed and joined his successful sons and their comrades on the château's southern steps. From

left (top row): Leutnant Carl Allmenröder (KiA 27 June 1917); Leutnant Lothar von Richthofen; Leutnant Wolfgang Plüschow (DoW 5 July 1918); Leutnant von Hartmann. (Bottom row): Leutnant Georg Simon (PoW 4 June 1917); Leutnant Kurt Wolff (KiA 15 September 1917); Manfred von Richthofen (KiA 21 April 1918); Major von Richthofen; Leutnant der Reserve Konstantin Krefft; Leutnant der Reserve Hans Hintsch (KiA 25 May 1917). Hauptmann Wilhelm Reinhard, who succeeded Manfred as Kommandeur of Jagdgeschwader I, recalled that the Major 'was called *der Fliegervater* [father of the flyers] by everyone in the Geschwader and rightfully so. His sons were two flying-heroes. The number of aerial victories of both of them reached the impressive height of 120 ... Father Richthofen also flew, not against the enemy, to be sure, but to visit his sons and, at that, not only once, but often. Such a visit was a day of honour for the Geschwader ... Despite his age [57], Father Richthofen placed himself at the disposal of the Nation; however, as he was partially deaf, he could no longer fight at the Front and became a garrison commander.'[20]

Opposite page top: Jagdstaffel 11 marked its move to Roucourt with three victories on 16 April. Leut-

nant Lothar von Richthofen shot down a Nieuport fighter that morning for his eighth confirmed claim; Vizefeldwebel Sebastian Festner also got a Nieuport in the same fight, which was logged as his 12th 'kill'; and late in the afternoon, Rittmeister Manfred von Richthofen shot down a B.E.2e, like the one seen here. Richthofen's description of his 45th triumph is the classic attack from above and behind, catching his opponent totally unawares: 'When ... flying just under the clouds, which were at an altitude of 1,000 metres, I observed an artillery flyer at 800 metres' altitude. I approached him unnoticed and attacked him, whereupon the aeroplane plunged downward smoking. The pilot caught the machine once more, but then lost control at 100 metres. The aeroplane plunged down between Bailleul and Gavrelle.' It is noteworthy that Richthofen's claim was accepted without question, even though the two-seater fell within British lines. Indeed, the B.E.2e from No. 13 Squadron, RFC, crashed only 25 kilometres from its airfield at Izel-les-Hameau. The pilot, Lieutenant Alphonso Pascoe, was wounded and sent back to England for treatment. Pascoe's observer, Second-Lieutenant Frederick S. Andrews, was more severely wounded and died thirteen days later.[21]

Right: Jagdstaffel 11 Albatros D.IIIs were joined by those of Jasta 4 to create this view of a massive array of German airpower at Roucourt. The photograph was widely circulated and, in this case, it appeared

on the cover of the weekly illustrated supplement to the Austrian *Tages-Post* of Linz. The Albatros in the foreground may have been flown by Richthofen's

technical officer, Leutnant der Reserve Konstantin Krefft.[22] Unmistakable behind it is Manfred von Richthofen's 'red bird' and third in line is Lothar's dark-coloured machine with the red band behind the cockpit. The fourth aeroplane appears to be one flown by Karl-Emil Schäfer.

Right: A key to Richthofen's success as a leader was his ability to draw subordinates and superiors to him. That quality was described by Hauptmann Erich von Salzmann, seen here (centre) during a visit to Roucourt in April: 'On one of those beautiful spring days in northern France we were standing on a street in Douai when a small rattletrap of a car came dashing toward us ... The car stopped. Two young officers got out; one in a short, open fur coat, hair askew, of medium height and solid, came up to me and said in clipped, military style: "Richthofen". So this was ... the airman who was beginning to become famous ... In my lifetime I have known very many people, [of whom] many remain in memory, many I have forgotten. At the time Richthofen was just at the beginning of his glorious rise, perhaps only one among many. Despite that, he caught my attention immediately. There was something in his bearing that created an especially pleasant impression. Richthofen possessed in large quantities that typically charming self-awareness and self-assurance, which must be innate, which one can never learn. In his face there was a calm, firm and yet friendly manliness, without any pronounced, determined tenseness, as found in many of our other young heroes ...'[23]

Opposite page, top: Richthofen's war trophies were set up in a room in the family home in Schweidnitz which later became a museum. The 'chandelier' (top centre) was made from a captured rotary engine. His earlier hunting trophies at the left – a boar's head and antlers from several stags – were overwhelmed by souvenirs from 'bigger game' – fabric bearing serial numbers taken from aeroplanes he had shot down. Left to right, top to bottom: 6997 – victory 18, Royal Aircraft Factory F.E.2b, No. 25 Squadron; A.1108 – victory 23, Sopwith 1½-Strutter, No. 43 Squadron;

6580 – victory 5, Royal Aircraft Factory B.E.12, No. 19 Squadron; 5841 – victory 32, Royal Aircraft Factory B.E.2d, No. 13 Squadron; A.6382 – victory 34, F.E.2d, No. 25 Squadron; 5986 – victory 12, Airco D.H.2, No. 32 Squadron; A.3340 – victory 36, Bristol F.2A, No. 48 Squadron; 7927 – victory 13, D.H.2, No. 29 Squadron; 4997 – victory 43, F.E.2b, No. 25 Squadron; 6580 – victory 5 (noted above); 6232 – victory 26, B.E.2d, No. 2 Squadron; 2506 – victory 8, B.E.2c, No. 12 Squadron; A.2401 – victory 33, Sopwith 1½-Strutter, No. 43 Squadron; 6997 – victory 18 (noted above); 6618 – victory 4, B.E.12, No. 21 Squadron; N.5193 – victory 16, Sopwith Pup, No. 8 Squadron, RNAS; 4997 – victory 43 (noted above); 5841 – victory 32 (noted above); 2506 – victory 8 (noted above); 5986 – victory 12, D.H.2, No. 32 Squadron; 9289(?) which matches none of Richthofen's claims; A.6382 – victory 34 (noted above); and another fabric swatch from the mysterious 9289(?).

Right: Richthofen's penchant for souvenirs inspired Leutnant Kurt Wolff to decorate a room in his home in similar fashion, as seen in this postcard photograph. Serial numbers of victims displayed on the

Leutnant Wolff

wall confirm Wolff's success in shooting down the following RFC aeroplanes in 1917: F.E.2b 7691 of No. 11 Squadron on 31 March (Lt L. A. T. Strange, PoW; 2/Lt William G. T. Clifton, DoW); R.E.8 A.3421 of No. 59 Squadron on 6 April (2/Lt A. Chaytor Pepper, PoW; Lt William L. Day, DoW); Bristol F.2A A.3338 of No. 48 Squadron on 11 April (Capt David M. Tidmarsh, MC, PoW; 2/Lt C. B. Holland, WiA/PoW). The enthusiasm to gather souvenirs was not matched by attention to the vanquished foe; Lieutenant Day has no known grave.[24] The fabric patch above Wolff's head presents a mystery. It reads '3469 TYPE 17', which indicates that it came from a French-built Nieuport, but the serial number does not match any of the Nieuport 17s he is known to have encountered.

Above: The colours and markings of Jagdstaffel 11 aeroplanes have long interested aviation historians. Leutnant Kurt Wolff's first Albatros was green (see page 39), but after the arrival of Albatros D.III D.632/17 on 19 April 1917, Wolff switched to a colour closer to that of his leader. His aeroplane is said to have been painted 'plum purple'[25] and, as seen in this photograph, Wolff copied Richthofen's colour scheme right down to the overpainted national marking. In the evening light on 1 May 1917, the aeroplane appeared to be red, according to comrades of the crew who became Wolff's 29th victim, Lieutenants G. S. French and G. P. Harding, MC, of No. 25 Squadron: 'Immediately after they had dropped their bombs, the formation was attacked from behind and above by nine hostile machines. Three hostile machines dived on Lieut. French's machine, which burst into flames, diving steeply ... 2/Lt [R. G.] Malcom was attacked and his engine was hit by a red scout that came up from underneath. He dived at once and Sgt [L.] Emsden shot it down. It was seen falling in flames by two officers of No. 16 Squadron and by the 1st Cavalry Division near Bois Bernard ...'[26] Despite the confirmations of downed

German aeroplanes, records show that this flight of F.E.2b bombers was attacked by Jasta 11, which reported no casualties that day. Wolff's manoeuvre after shooting down one aeroplane was most likely intended to fool his adversaries.

Opposite page, bottom: Manfred von Richthofen appears rigid and apprehensive in this postcard photograph with Generalleutnant Ernst von Hoeppner, Commanding General of the Air Force, taken at Roucourt at the end of April. Having surpassed the record of his mentor, Oswald Boelcke, Richthofen was being thrust into greater prominence as a national figure and had not yet become fully accustomed to it. There was no question, however, that he had earned the highest respect of General von Hoeppner, who later wrote: 'Above all, in the first weeks of April the air combats of the Jagdstaffeln developed into the first aerial battles. The opponent attacked our aeroplanes with the greatest courage and in the face of substantially numerically superior forces. But he paid for his attack lust with severest casualties; the 6th of April saw 44 enemy aeroplanes shot down by the firepower of our superiorly armed and systematically directed Jagdstaffeln. To be sure, we also suffered painful losses of proven fighter pilots. But, above all, Jagdstaffel 11, led by Freiherr von Richthofen, distinguished itself. In the period from 23 January to 22 April 1917, they attained a hundred confirmed aerial victories. Boelcke's spirit lived in them.'[27]

Right: Richthofen (second from left) appears more relaxed when introducing General von Hoeppner to one of his most successful pupils, Leutnant Karl-Emil Schäfer, and other comrades (from left): Leutnant von Hartmann; Leutnant der

Reserve Konstantin Krefft; Leutnant der Reserve Otto Brauneck; Leutnant Lothar Freiherr von Richthofen; Leutnant der Reserve Hans Hintsch. At far left is Hauptmann Maximillian Sorg, 6. Armee's Officer in Charge of Aviation. Schäfer's career was advancing swiftly, as he wrote with playful pride to his parents on 26 April: 'Today is an eventful day, which I am celebrating with the most intense emotions. His Majesty the Kaiser has deigned to present Leutnant Schäfer with the Knight's Cross of the most exalted Order of the House of Hohenzollern. That is the purely gratifying part. In addition, an order from the Commanding General of the Air Force mentioned: "Leutnant Schäfer will be appointed leader of Jagdstaffel 28." That makes me happy. And I am proud that I have been appointed directly as [Staffel] leader, not starting as deputy leader. But I am bitterly sad that I must leave the Staffel I have come to love, the splendid circle of comrades and, most of all, Richthofen. If I had a choice, I would prefer a thousand times more to remain here. It is a consolation that at least Jagdstaffel 28 still flies against the Englishmen.'[28] The same day Schäfer became the first Richthofen protégé to be awarded the *Orden Pour le Mérite*.[29]

Below: Lothar von Richthofen was superstitious and particularly feared the number 13, even though his 13th victory was achieved by incredibly good luck. At midday on Sunday, 29 April 1917, Lothar joined his brother Manfred and Kurt Wolff in an attack on three SPAD S.7s of No. 19 Squadron near Lécluse, east of Arras. Manfred and Wolff sent their opponents crashing to their deaths.[30] Lothar, who had run out of ammunition, used another tactic to force down his adversary. He recounted: 'I forced the Englishman to turn again and again. Turning in aerial combat brings one lower and lower until one must land or attempt to fly directly home. My Englishman decided on the latter ... At the required distance, about 50 metres, I aimed cleanly and pressed my machine-gun buttons [on the control column]. What's this! Not a shot came out ... I looked at my machine-guns. Damn it all! I had fired every last shot. I had empty ammunition belts in my hand.'[31] In desperation Lothar flew closer and closer to the SPAD, whose pilot looked back, ready to face the *coup de grâce*. When no final shot came, Lieutenant W. N. Hamilton landed before Lothar's propeller could chew up the SPAD's rudder, and send down both aeroplanes. Lothar examined the SPAD a little while later and was chagrined to

find that he had expended 1,000 rounds without putting a single hole in the British fighter.

Opposite page, top: That Lothar learned a lesson from his encounter with the SPAD was demonstrated that evening north-east of Monchy-le-Preux. Holding his fire until the right moment, he shot down a two-seater.[32] Over nearby Roeux, Manfred had just finished off a B.E.2c[33] like the one seen here, and recorded his brother's achievement with pride: 'While I observed [the location of] the shell-hole into which my opponent crashed, I looked over at [Lothar]. He was barely 500 metres away from me and still fighting with his adversary. I had time to witness this scene in detail and I must say that I could not have done better myself. He had caught the opponent unawares and they were circling each other. Then suddenly the enemy aeroplane reared up – a sure sign of being hit, surely the pilot had been shot in the head or something similar – the aeroplane dived and the wings of the enemy machine folded up one after the other. The wreckage fell in the vicinity of my [51st] victim. I flew over to my brother and ... we waved at each other. We were satisfied and flew on.'[34]

Opposite page, bottom: On 29 April Manfred shot down four aeroplanes. The last one of the day – his 52nd – was a Sopwith Triplane of the type seen here in German hands. Shortly after the Richthofen brothers had dealt with the two-seaters, eleven Sopwith Triplanes and a Nieuport 17 stalked the German formation from above. 'Finally, one of them got up his courage and dropped down on our man at the rear,' Richthofen wrote. 'Of course, the challenge was accepted, even though it was unfavourable for us, for he who attacks from above has the advantage. But when there are no other customers, one must take what one can get. Therefore we turned in our tracks. The Englishmen noticed this and immediately broke off. But the beginning had been made. Another Englishman tried to do the same thing. He had sought me out as an opponent and I greeted him with a salvo from both machine-guns. He did not seem to

like that. He tried to get away from me by diving. That was his ruination, for in so doing he was below me ... Whatever is beneath me, where possible all alone and over our territory, is as good as lost, especially when it is a single-seater, a fighter that cannot shoot from the rear. The opponent had a very good machine and was very fast. But he did not succeed in reaching his lines.'[35] Relentlessly Richthofen pursued his quarry and sent it down to a fiery fatal crash.

Right: Next day Richthofen received the supreme compliment for his achievements, a telegram from the Kaiser. Dated 29 April, the message offered adulation rarely accorded to a junior officer: 'It has been

reported to Me that you have emerged victorious in aerial combat for the 50th time. I express to you for this magnificent success My hearty congratulations

and My fullest appreciation. The Fatherland looks upon its brave flyers with admiration and gratitude. May God continue to be with you. Wilhelm I. R.'

Below: Richthofen maintained his 'Red Baron' image even in routine flying. Most air units had a 'hack' aeroplane for behind-the-lines flights and, appropriately, Jagdstaffel 11 had the all-red Albatros C.IX two-seater seen here. Typically, Richthofen was helped into a heavy flying-suit by one of the ground-crew, while the other (right) held his helmet and goggles. Richthofen used the two-seater to return to Germany for his first leave since taking command of Jasta 11. This came about as the result of a telephone call after he had received the Kaiser's telegram: 'In the evening ... the telephone rang and nothing less than [someone at] "Supreme Headquarters" wished to speak to me. It was quite a bit of fun to be connected with the "great shack". Among other things I received the delightful news that His Majesty expressed the wish to speak with me personally and the day was already set: the 2nd of May. This [information] reached me on the 30th of April at 9 p.m. It would not be possible to go by train to comply with the wish of the Supreme Warlord. So it was better to ... travel by the aerial route. The next morning I took off and, to be sure, not in my single-seater, "*Le petit rouge*", but, rather, in a big, fat two-seater.'[36]

4 — A Commander of Steel-Hard Will

Below: Manfred von Richthofen's return to Germany was a momentous event. Alighting from the red Albatros C.IX in Cologne, he was greeted by a crowd of officers, keen to be seen and photographed with Germany's greatest living fighter ace. Notice that the officer at the right, wearing an Observer's Badge on his tunic, also sports his dress sword, as does the officer second from left. But from the time Manfred turned over command of Jagdstaffel 11 to his brother Lothar and departed Roucourt, he began to unwind from the tensions of combat and organisational formality. 'I sat in the back [of the two-seater], that is, not at the "joystick". The work was done by Leutnant Krefft, one of the gentlemen of my Jagdstaffel,' Richthofen wrote. 'He wanted to go on recuperative leave, therefore [the flight] suited him just fine. He would get home quicker ... My departure was head over heels. I could take nothing more than a toothbrush with me in the aeroplane, [and] therefore I had to appear at Supreme Headquarters dressed as I was. In the field even a professional soldier does not have much in the way of beautiful items of clothing; in any case, not a poor front-line swine like myself.'[1]

Right: The three-hour flight from Roucourt to Cologne gave Richthofen a headache and he took a nap prior to the next leg of the trip, to the spa city of Bad Kreuznach. But he did not set out before spending time with people who regarded him as a great hero. He tried to appear nonchalant about his emerging status, but let slip bursts of enthusiasm and a bit of self-importance in his autobiography *Der rote Kampfflieger* (The Red Battle-Flyer), which he began writing during this period of home-leave: 'Someone had announced [our flight to] Cologne and we were expected there. The day before, news of my 52nd victory had appeared in the newspapers. So the reception was held accordingly ... We arrived at Supreme Headquarters in the afternoon and were greeted warmly by some comrades I knew who

worked in the "Great Shack". I felt truly sorry for these pencil-pushers. They have only half the fun of war. Next, I reported to the Commanding General of the Air Force [Generalleutnant von Hoeppner].

Next morning came the great moment when I was presented to [Generalfeldmarschall] von Hindenburg and [his chief of staff, General von] Ludendorff.'[2] One of those 'pencil-pushers' was Richthofen's friend Oberleutnant Fritz von Falkenhayn, who relieved Leutnant Konstantin Krefft of flying the celebrated airfighter to other appointments.

Left: The marble and bronze bust of Kaiser Wilhelm II (centre), seen in the Richthofen Museum in Schweidnitz, was the monarch's 25th birthday present to the ace. Following Richthofen's meetings with the stern and imposing von Hindenburg and von Ludendorff on

2 May 1917, he went on to a more pleasant experience. 'It is an unreal feeling to be in the room where the fate of the world is decided. So I was quite happy when I left the "Great Shack" behind me and, at midday, was commanded to have breakfast with His Majesty [the Kaiser]. It was my birthday and someone divulged that to His Majesty and he congratulated me. Once for my success, then for the 25th year of my life. He also surprised me with a small birthday present. Earlier, I would never have dreamed that I would sit to the right of Hindenburg and be mentioned in a speech by the Field Marshal.'[3]

Above: The city of Bad Kreuznach was virtually taken over by the government to provide the Kaiser and the General Staff with a western command post within Germany. Consequently, the Kaiserin (Empress) and her entourage took up residence in the nearby spas of Bad Homburg vor der Höhe, which maintained their pre-war charm and comforts. The day after his meeting with the Kaiser, Richthofen was flown by Oberleutnant Fritz von Falkenhayn in the Aviatik C.II seen here to meet Kaiserin Auguste Viktoria (centre). Manfred related details of the meeting to Lothar, who wrote: 'The Kaiserin had such interest in aviation that she appeared at the airfield. For flying my brother had on the old leather coat he wore when he achieved all his victories. Right after landing he presented himself to the Kaiserin. In order to clarify, as it were, why he had to wear the old leather coat to this ceremonious occasion, he told her that he had achieved 52 aerial victories while wearing it. The Kaiserin touched the coat gently and said: "The good coat has been with you for 52 aerial victories."'[4]

Right: Richthofen was not completely out of uniform while visiting Germany's royal family. He did not have with him the full dress uniform seen on page 10, but under his leather coat he was wearing the traditional Uhlan's tunic bearing enough important awards to be recognisable: Iron Cross 2nd Class ribbon on the right-side row of buttons, Iron Cross 1st Class medal and Military Pilot's Badge on the left side, and, at his collar, the blue and gold badge of the *Orden Pour le Mérite*. His friend Fritz Falkenhayn, scion of a noble military family dating back to the 16th century,[5] wore a ribbons bar in lieu of seven decorations and the Iron Cross 1st Class, the Duchy of Oldenburg's Friedrich August Cross 1st Class and Military Pilot's Badge pinned to his tunic. Falkenhayn had begun his career with an élite guards grenadier regiment, but switched to aviation as an observer in 1913 and became a pilot the following year.[6] On 27 November 1914, he was appointed adjutant to the Fliegerkorps of the German Supreme High Command. Falkenhayn admired and, as much as possible, supported Richthofen within the upper echelons of the German military command.

Below: After meeting the Kaiserin, Richthofen relived old times by flying in the back seat of this Albatros

C.III at Flieger-Ersatz-Abteilung 7 in Cologne. In view of his value as a national figure, he was told to use ground transportation while in Germany, but in Bad Kreuznach he was unimpressed by the protection accorded to heroes and bent the rules. He met Kapitän zur See (Naval Captain) Nicholas Count zu Dohna-Schlodien, the highly decorated former commander of the surface raider SMS *Möwe*, who had become the Kaiser's aide-de-camp, and knew that such a 'safe' staff position was not for him. When asked about being forbidden to fly on the Kaiser's orders, Richthofen replied: 'That [prohibition] goes only so far. After I had attained my 30th [victory], His Majesty said to me: "I do not want to hear that you are still flying!" Then, when I came back after the 50th, His Majesty wagged his finger at me [and said]: "I have heard that you have been flying again. Be careful that nothing happens to you." And during the last visit, His Majesty turned to [Count zu Dohna-Schlodien] and said: "How could that be? Have I not forbidden him to fly?" The aide replied: "Majesty, in

the interests of the whole situation we cannot do that. We need Richthofen as an example and as a Geschwader-Kommandeur [Air Wing Commander], we need him as a combat pilot ..."'[7] And that was just what Richthofen wanted to be.

Above: Freed from official duties, Richthofen spent enjoyable hours among newcomers to aviation. He flew in several trainers, including this 1915-vintage Rumpler C.I; close examination of the forward cockpit shows the Rumpler's steering-wheel controls, a hallmark of outmoded early military aeroplanes. Richthofen's method of travel may have surprised neophyte pilots at FEA 7, but reinforced basic points of his own training syllabus for all men new to combat flying: 'I place little significant value on the skill of flying itself. I shot down my first 20 [victims] when I still had the greatest difficulty with flying itself. It does not matter whether one is an aerobatic artist. Furthermore, I prefer [someone] who can fly only in left-hand turns – but who goes after the enemy – to the diving and turning specialist from [the training centre at] Johannisthal, who attacks too cautiously.'[8]

Below: Richthofen's circle of influential friends grew quickly and he astutely maintained the contacts. During his stop-over in Cologne, he chatted pleasantly with Hauptmann Otto Zimmer-Vorhaus, a pre-war aviator who, on 25 September 1916, assembled the first Jagdstaffel.[9] Zimmer-Vorhaus, then 6. Armee's Staff Officer in Charge of Aviation, had previously made Feldflieger-Abteilung 18 into such a strong unit that Richthofen and other Jasta leaders often requested its most aggressive pilots for their own Staffeln. One of the German Air Force's forward thinkers, Zimmer-Vorhaus later established in Cologne the training unit for *Riesenflugzeuge* (giant bombers) that attacked distant targets.[10] Zimmer-Vorhaus' leadership and organisational influence showed in Richthofen's admonition to his men:

'Everyone must show absolute trust in the leader in the air. If this trust is lacking, success is impossible from the outset. The Staffel gains trust by [the leader's] exemplary daring and the conviction that [he] sees everything and is able to cope with every situation.'[11]

Above: Ludicrous news appeared on 4 May 1917, as Richthofen and Krefft (second from right) set out for a hunting vacation in the Black Forest. German newspapers reported the formation of a special British air unit to shoot down or capture Richthofen and record the event on film. Its accuracy never verified, the article claimed that the British pilot who downed Germany's top-scoring fighter ace would receive the Victoria Cross, a promotion, £5,000 and various valuable gifts.[12] Richthofen made light of the account: 'How would it be if the situation were reversed? How would it be if I were to shoot down the British squadron? Would I then receive the Victoria Cross, a promotion, my own aeroplane as a gift, £5,000 and a special prize from the manufacturer whose aeroplane I use? I am easily satisfied. I want only to get the cameraman who is supposed to film me being shot down. That I want very much!'[13]

Opposite page, top: Continuing problems with Albatros D.III fighters led Manfred to the test facility at Adlershof, outside Berlin, before going home at the end of his leave. On 16 May he tested an LFG Roland

D.III to compare it with the Albatros he flew at the Front. The sleek, plywood-fuselaged LFG Roland was similar in construction to the Albatros, but disappointing in overall performance. Richthofen was assured by Albatros company officials that new, improved machines were coming and older models were being upgraded by factory mechanics in the field. Indeed, he was proud of his brother Lothar's swiftly mounting success in the Albatros, including a particularly arduous scrap during a rainstorm on 7 May. Although Lothar crashed at the end of the encounter, he was credited with his 20th 'kill', said to be the celebrated British ace Captain Albert Ball, DSO, MC. After a brief visit to Schweidnitz, Manfred wrote to his mother: 'Toward the end of [May] I will tour the other Fronts in the Balkans, etc. That will take about three to four weeks. Meanwhile, Lothar leads my Staffel and will indeed be the

next [fighter pilot] to receive the *Pour le Mérite*. What do you say now about both of your wayward sons?'[14]

Below: Just as Manfred had once sought out Oswald Boelcke to learn about aerial combat, in mid-May 1917 he himself was approached by the promising fighter pilot Oberleutnant Hans Bethge (right). He was more than a year older than Richthofen and had shot down

an enemy aeroplane earlier in his career than had Richthofen, but Bethge was glad to mention that he too was a veteran of the *Brieftauben-Abteilung Ostende* for the opportunity of discussing leadership and air combat techniques with Boelcke's successor. At the time of this meeting, Bethge had five confirmed victories to his credit and was the leader of Jagdstaffel 30, established in January 1917. He was on leave in Berlin and, judging by the account of his fourth victory, he had much to learn: 'I wanted to attack the last one in the formation, but three turned towards me and then began the wildest battle that I have ever had in the air. Machines whizzed past each other ... seven Nieuports, quite new machines, against two Albatroses. Loops, sideslips, bizarre twists, attacks and escapes and attacks in frantic rushes. Well, then I slipped 300 metres ... [but] struggled back up again and then saw a Nieuport just over the lines and attacked it.'[15] No doubt guided by Richthofen's advice, Bethge refined his technique and went on to shoot down a total of 20 aeroplanes. He was killed in combat the day before the *Pour le Mérite* was to be awarded to him.[16]

Below: The realisation that he too was mortal was brought home to Manfred when Lothar crashed after shooting down his 24th victim. Publicly, Manfred played down the hip wound that required his brother

to be hospitalised, but he headed for home to spend time with his mother and sister Ilse. He mistakenly thought that by arriving on an early Saturday train, he could slip into Schweidnitz unnoticed, but his life had changed and crowds, like the one seen here, gathered wherever he appeared. His mother recalled that on 19 May 'at 7 a.m., Ilse met him at the train. They came back by foot. Scarcely had the news of his arrival [begun to] spread when a flood of floral arrangements and small gifts poured down on us. The entire city seems to have been mobilised. I knew how very reluctant Manfred was to be honoured like this. But there was nothing else to do and he found himself in this role reluctantly. There was no shortage of tributes, neither from the *Wandervogel* [Bird of Passage youth movement] with the sing-song whirring of their lutes nor from the nursery school children with paper helmets and tassels.'[17]

Below: The outpouring of public support and pride continued. 'The beautiful weather on Sunday encouraged the crowds to come to our home,' Freifrau von Richthofen wrote. 'At times the street [in front of the house] was filled with people. We spent the whole day in the garden. Delegations came and went ... and again I see how Manfred spends time with the children; how they are devoted to him, how it gives him such joy to

look into so many young faces glowing with enthusiasm.'[18] A few days later the Richthofen women whisked Manfred off to the countryside to escape the crowds. In a quiet place, he told them about his experiences in Bad Kreuznach, which only reinforced his mother's opinion: 'Manfred was glad to have [the visit to] the Supreme Headquarters behind him. For him, a dedicated front-line soldier, such receptions as the one he was ordered to attend on 1 May, are no source of edification. He was no friend of the rarified air of the Royal Court and [as he remarked with an exaggerated groan] completely unsuited for the profession of aide-de-camp. He longed for the roar of the propeller, the clatter of the machine-gun, the austere but vigorous life with his comrades out there in the barracks and tents ... That was in his nature.'[19]

Right: After this rest – which included several hunting trips – Richthofen headed for his next assignment at the end of May. He and his orderly, Menzke, set out on an extensive tour of aviation facilities in Austria and Turkey. He knew that, like Boelcke before him, he was being sent away for safe-keeping, as in the visit to the Austrian testing station at Aspern, seen here. With Lothar still in hospital, it would not do to have something happen to the senior brother. When Richthofen learned that his protégé Leutnant Karl-

Emil Schäfer had been killed in combat on 5 June, however, he cancelled the remainder of the tour and headed back to Germany for the funeral. Dead at the age of 25, Schäfer had shot down 30 enemy aeroplanes, received the *Pour le Mérite* and was leading his own unit, Jasta 28w, when he was killed by the two-seater crew whom he anticipated would be his 31st victory. As Richthofen learned upon returning to Berlin, his 23-year-old cousin Leutnant Oskar von Schickfuss und Neudorff, a pilot with Jasta 3, had been killed over British lines within hours of Schäfer's death. Both men had been flying Albatros D.IIIs, which raised anew questions about the Albatros' reliability in combat.

ALBATROSS NIEUPORT

Left: Germany's first-line fighter was no mystery to the Royal Flying Corps. The day before Schäfer and Schickfuss were killed, Jasta 11's Leutnant Georg Simon had encountered Nieuport 17s of No. 29 Squadron, RFC and had his engine put out of action by their flight commander, Captain Charles M. B. Chapman. Unable to get back to his own lines, he was forced to land his Albatros D.III intact within Allied lines at Fontaine-lès-Croisilles, near Arras, the fifth of Chapman's seven confirmed victories.[20] The captured aeroplane was assigned the reference number G 42, later fitted with the engine of a captured newer Albatros D.III and test flown in England.[21]

Right: A two-seater was provided for Richthofen's flight to Karl-Emil Schäfer's hometown. Writing to his mother, the strong-willed air warrior made a point of mentioning that he was flying – not being flown – back to his airfield at the Front: 'I attended Schäfer's funeral. I flew from Berlin to Krefeld in two hours; it would have taken eight hours by train. I took Herr von Salzmann with me and he was very excited by his first flight.'[22] Richthofen seems to have regarded Erich von Salzmann as a mentor, and the former army officer turned journalist evidenced equally high regard for his young friend. 'One of the nicest experiences in my life was associated with Richthofen: I flew with him,' Salzmann wrote, noting how his friend maintained his composure, even while travelling to a funeral. 'And yet, once

again it was the same, the forms in which the young nobleman officer was trained clung to him as closely as his own skin. One perceived in him the [ways of the] cadets, not in some sort of overdone strictness, or in clipped speech that waited until the older person had spoken. No! Rather, again and again, in every difficult-to-define, superb mannerism, in gesture, in speaking, in his whole appearance, he was always in control of himself. Yet, he always had a friendly smile on his lips.'[23]

Opposite page, bottom: Before returning to the Front, Richthofen was invited back to Supreme Headquarters where he was greeted by Generalfeldmarschall von Hindenburg (centre). The visit was overshadowed by other personal events, as seen in Richthofen's letter of 18 June: 'Arrived back here and hard at work. Have just shot down No. 53. In Bad Kreuznach, I was again invited to be with His Majesty, where I met the King of Bulgaria, who presented me with the Cross of Bravery 1st Class. It is worn just like the Iron Cross 1st Class and looks very nice. I met the Reichs-Chancellor ... and some other ministers.

'About Oskar [von Schickfuss und Neudorff] I have been able to determine with certainty that he is in fact dead, for he fell or jumped from his aeroplane [during] the last 500 metres. He lies near the Front, but on the other side ...

'Yesterday, unfortunately, [Leutnant Georg] Zeumer fell in aerial combat. Perhaps it was best for him, for he knew the end of his life was just ahead of him. This splendid pleasant fellow! It would have been terrible if he had to be tormented to death slowly. So this was a beautiful hero's death.'[24]

Below: By the time Richthofen returned to Jasta 11, the unit had been re-equipped with what was heralded as an improved Albatros D.V. The cockpit of the new Albatros, seen here, was little changed from that of its predecessor; indeed, the D.V did not perform better and continued to suffer from the wing failures linked to the D.III model.[25] Richthofen soon became disillusioned with the D.V and complained to his friend Oberleutnant Fritz von Falkenhayn, the Technical Officer on the staff of the Commanding General of the Air Force: 'Our aeroplanes, quite frankly, are ridiculously inferior to the British. The [Sopwith] Triplane and 200hp SPAD, as well as the Sopwith [Camel] single-seater, play with our Albatros D.V ... The D.V is so far surpassed and so ridiculously inferior to the British single-seaters that one cannot begin to do anything with [the D.V]. But the [aeroplane manufacturers] at home have brought out no new machines for almost a year, [only] these lousy Albatroses, and [we] have remained stuck with the Albatros D.IIIs in which I fought in the autumn of last year.'[26]

Left: On 10 June, Jagdstaffel 11 changed airfields from Roucourt in France on 6. Armee's front to Bavichove in Belgium, north-east of Courtrai (now Kortrijk), on 4. Armee's front. Manfred von Richthofen seems to be lost in thought as he walks about the new airfield, testing the ground for soft spots with his walking-stick (visible lower left). From his recent visit to the Supreme High Command, he knew that a major organisational change was to be announced, as General von Hoeppner recalled: 'The ever-increasing number of aeroplanes which the opposition were deploying to reach a target made it seem desirable for us to combine several Jagdstaffeln into a Jagdgeschwader [Fighter Wing] ... and in the personage of Rittmeister von Richthofen ... [it] received a commander whose steel-hard will and in relentlessly pursuing the enemy was infused in every member of the Geschwader.'[27] On 23 June 1917, Richthofen was appointed Kommandeur of Germany's first fighter wing – Jagdgeschwader I – composed of Jagdstaffeln 4, 6, 10 and 11. He was succeeded as leader of Jasta 11 by one of his most successful former pupils, Leutnant Kurt Wolff, who was then a 31-victory ace and recipient of the *Pour le Mérite*.

Opposite page, bottom: Land-based German naval air units in Flanders operated near the seaward edge of 4. Armee's front and, as part of his new responsibilities, Richthofen familiarised himself with their facilities. Photographs of the period show that he used various Albatros D.Vs. Here a naval air mechanic checks out the cockpit of one of them – 4693/17 – while the Kommandeur is deep in conversation with an army pilot. The naval officer second from right appears to be looking at the all-red rudder with the national marking over-painted in the manner of Richthofen's earlier Albatros. This aeroplane was very likely the one in which Richthofen was wounded and forced to land on 6 July (see photograph on page 74).

Above: For a courtesy call at another naval air unit – this time II. Marine-Feldflieger-Abteilung – Richthofen flew an Albatros D.V with the forward fuselage painted red up to the windscreen. He ensured that

his personal aeroplanes were well marked with his identifying colour and would be easily recognised by his own pilots and those of neighbouring units. Even at this early stage, plans were being developed for a joint Army-Navy operation in Flanders – code-named *Unternehmen Strandfest* (Operation 'Beach Party')[28] – and JG I pilots were to work closely with their naval counterparts. Richthofen was in hospital when the mission took place in driving rain on 12 July, but his part in the planning contributed to success of the operation.[29]

Left: On 24 June 1917, the new Kommandeur showed that, despite having an inferior aeroplane, a determined fighter pilot could still do his job. His 55th victim was an Airco D.H.4,[30] like the wrecked machine seen here with German groundcrew considering the fate of the 'luckless' flyers. This D.H.4 was his 38th two-seater 'kill' to date, which showed that the defeat of a 2-man crew had less to do with luck than drawing on his own experience. 'In the beginning I fought ... as an observer in so-called two-seat combat aeroplanes without success, and then in spring 1916 as a pilot in the same type of aeroplane. I like to refer to that time as really being my instruction period ... In these aerial combats I learned the characteristics of the opponents, as well as of our own aeroplanes. I learned in two-seaters that one must be especially defensive in order not to be shot down. In addition, I flew from time to time in a Fokker [single-seater], in which one cannot fly defensively; rather one must fly only offensively. For this reason [I conclude that] a careful pilot can never be a fighter pilot. The careful pilot will at all times fight defensively and therefore never shoot down [an opponent], as, if I were in a two-seater with a machine-gunner in the back seat, I would be in a good position to shoot down an adversary.'[31]

Below: Manfred's next two victories – Nos. 56 and 57 – were R.E.8 observation aeroplanes, of the type seen here, from No. 53 Squadron.[32] Those seeking to play down the Richthofen legend often take the erroneous view that such slow, ungainly two-seaters were 'easy' targets for a skilled fighter pilot such as Richthofen. In fact, armed with two machine-guns, a well-coordinated observer and pilot team could be formidable

opponents. Hence, Richthofen pounced on these two R.E.8s and dispatched the observers as quickly as possible. 'Aerial combat is an area that one can really sum up in a single sentence,' Richthofen wrote. 'I once asked Boelcke about his tactic. Then I was a complete newcomer and had not yet shot down any aeroplanes. He answered me: "I go after one and aim for a clean shot!" I was irritated that he had not revealed his secret and flew back home. But now I know that with that [sentence] Boelcke had revealed his tactic.'[33]

Left: On 2 July 1917, the successor to Boelcke's legacy settled into spacious new quarters at Château de Béthune in Marcke (now Marke), south-west of Courtrai. As he was not a member of Silesia's landed aristocracy, Richthofen had no ancestral home and surely marvelled at this castle, built in 1802 by a family that had distinguished itself in the Napoleonic Wars. The glories of history were not allowed to interfere with his mission, however, as recorded by Geschwader adjutant Karl Bodenschatz: 'The Kommandeur invited all the leaders of the [four] Jagdstaffeln to a meeting in his room on the second floor [of the castle]. Everything was still barren and unpleasant. Moreover, not all the rooms of the castle were at our disposal because the ... lord of the manor here wanted most of all to blow up this whole flying business and, as this was not possible, at least he exploded every polite contact with his sullen lack of friendliness and locked up as many rooms as possible. The Rittmeister watched this inhospitable business patiently for a few days and then had it changed.'[34]

Below: An aerial photograph of Marcke shows that Baron Jean de Béthune's manor house (A) at the end of Kasteeldreef (Castle Lane) and its adjacent lawns provided a comfortable base for half of Jagdgeschwader I. The large flat area between Kasteeldreef and Bissegemstraat (road to Bisseghem) became Jasta 11's airfield (B) and an orderly room (C) was established in a private house along the road to Courtrai, Kortrijkstraat No. 74, a short walk from the château. Jasta 4's airfield was north-west of the château (D) and Jasta 6 set up its operations just across the river Lys (E). Initially Jasta 10 was at Heule airfield, north of Jasta 4, but, to be more available for joint air operations, the Staffel soon moved to Marcke. Once the units settled in, Bodenschatz wrote: 'The assembled Geschwader looked extremely colourful. The *Stammstaffel* [core unit], Jasta 11, with which Richthofen flew, had their machines painted red; Jasta 10 [used] yellow; Jasta 6 had zebra stripes; and Jasta 4 bore a black snake line along the natural wood-finished fuselage ...'[35]

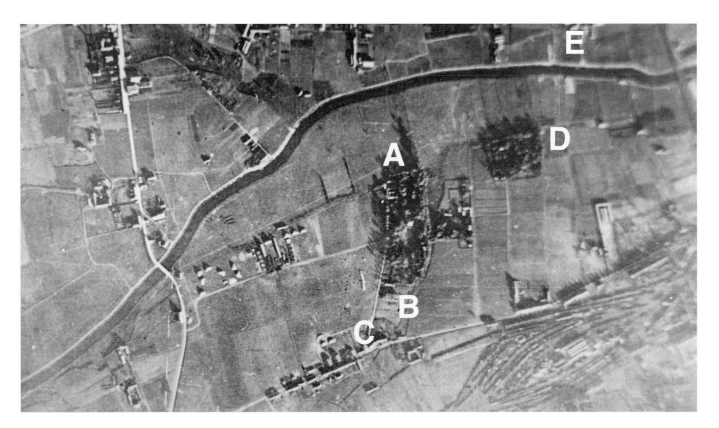

Above: During JG I's first extensive operations on 6 July, Richthofen flew Albatros D.V 4693/17, of which only the nose, wheel covers and tail were red. It is seen here after he had made a forced landing in it and was nearly killed. In response to a report that British low-level attack aeroplanes were heading for the Front, Richthofen flew with Jasta 11 to head them off. Before they could reach their intended targets, however, the Germans spotted a flight of F.E.2d two-seat bombers and attacked them. Richthofen trained his gunsight on the rearmost and approached in his usual determined fashion, looking to eliminate the observer and then shoot into the cockpit area until the aeroplane fell. 'Then I watched as the observer, in great excitement, fired at me,' Richthofen wrote later. 'I calmly let him shoot, for even the best sharpshooter's marksmanship could not help at a distance of 300 metres. One just does not hit!' As he recounted, seconds later his scoffing proved to be premature: 'Suddenly there was a blow to my head! I was hit! For a moment I was completely paralysed ... The worst part was that the blow on the head affected my optic nerve and I was completely blinded. The machine dived down.'[36]

Opposite page, top left: By great luck, his temporary blindness passed and he regained control of his aeroplane. Two comrades recognised his difficulties and broke off to protect the Kommandeur until he set down in a field of high grass near Wervicq, Belgium. German troops in the area summoned help and he was taken to St. Nicholas' Hospital in Courtrai. As this view of his flying-helmet shows, he sustained a serious head wound, which he described casually: 'I had quite a respectable hole in my head, a wound of about ten centimetres across [in] which ... in one place clear white bone as big as a *Taler* [large coin] remained exposed. My thick Richthofen head had once again proved itself. The skull had not been penetrated. With some imagination, in the X-ray

photographs one could notice a slight swelling. It was a skull fracture that I was not rid of for days, [and] was not very comfortable.' Historians have long thought that Richthofen was shot down by his intended victim, Second Lieutenant Albert E. Woodbridge, an observer with No. 20 Squadron. Examination of the medical records,[37] however, show that the wound was above and slightly behind his left ear – making it more likely that he was hit from behind, inadvertently, by one of his comrades.

Above right: As Richthofen recovered from surgery performed by Obergeneralarzt (Major-General in the Medical Corps) Prof. Dr. Kraske,[38] his comrades waged a war of words with a tenacious nurse. JG I Adjutant Karl Bodenschatz, accompanied by the leaders of Jastas 4, 6 and 11– Oberleutnant Kurt-Bertram von Döring, Oberleutnant Eduard Dostler and Leutnant Kurt Wolff – had rushed to the hospital in Courtrai to talk to their Kommandeur. But nurse Käte Otersdorf was determined that her patient should rest and stopped them at the door. Finally, Bodenschatz persuaded her that a brief visit would not adversely affect Richthofen's progress. He described the scene: 'Nurse Käte stares angrily at the foolish visitors [and] then goes inside [the room]. When she returns, the four may go in. With a thick snow-white bandage around his head, the Rittmeister receives them rather dejectedly. "I am so sorry", he says, "to stay away now, right in the middle of everything, but I will come back soon, very soon." He has a ten-centimetre-long wound on his head, [which] could be stitched together, but later on one place in his hair one always saw the bare, white skullbone gleaming out. But ... everything goes well. Richthofen's father, who is the local commandant in the Lille area, has been notified and his mother, as well. Command of the Geschwader has been assumed by Oberleutnant von Döring.'[39]

5 — Frail Mortality

Below: The absence of Manfred von Richthofen's famous red Albatros for six weeks was a successfully guarded secret. Neither the German popular press nor Allied intelligence[1] reported how close the 57-victory ace had come to being killed. The weekly report of the Commanding General of the Air Force listed as German casualties for 6 July 1917: 'Two aeroplanes lost (both over enemy lines) in combat; one aeroplane has not returned; three aeroplanes [forced down, but] not due to enemy action. In addition five officers, two non-commissioned officers wounded.'[2] Even 4. Armee's Officer in Charge of Aviation reported in routine fashion: 'Rttmstr.Frhr.v. Richthofen, lightly wounded in aerial combat.'[3] Nor did the late 1917 edition of Richthofen's autobiography *Der rote Kampfflieger* mention his perilous encounter with the British two-seaters between Comines and Warneton. A post-war compilation of his writings included an account which ended on a note of bravado: 'It was reported at home that I lay in the hospital with severe head and abdominal

wounds. I was curious as to who would climb into an [aeroplane] first, my brother or I. My brother feared it would be me and I feared it would be my brother.'[4]

Right: Five days after Richthofen was forced down, he was joined in the same hospital by Jagdstaffel 11 leader Leutnant Kurt Wolff (centre front row), who was wearing a sling to support his injured left wrist. He had been surprised by the quick strike tactic he himself used so effectively and, although he claimed that fifteen enemy aeroplanes overwhelmed his formation of seven, British records[5] show that four Airco D.H.5s of No. 32 Squadron attacked the Jasta 11 flight. Wolff was most likely the third of ten confirmed victories scored by [then] Lieutenant St. Cyprian C. Tayler, a 22-year-old South African who was to perish eight months later. Wolff's letter to his fiancée, Maria Martha Bömeleit, treated the incident cavalierly: 'Yesterday morning ... I held my hand where an Englishman was shooting and the hand turned away ever so slightly as the bullet attempted to hit it, but the bullet being the harder part, it went through the hand. Therefore I have a clean shot through the left hand, [and] the wrist bone was shot clean through ... '[6] Gathered for this photograph when the two wounded airmen visited Château de Béthune are, top row from left: Leutnant Eberhard Mohnike; Oberleutnant Wilhelm Reinhard; Nurse Käte Weinstroth; Manfred von Richthofen; Major Albrecht von Richthofen; Oberleutnant Kurt Scheffer. Middle row: Leut-

Leutnant der Reserve Karl Meyer; Leutnant Carl August von Schönebeck.

Below: A gathering of a different sort took place when Jagdgeschwader I members posed with the acting Kommandeur, Oberleutnant Kurt-Bertram von Döring (middle, striking a profile pose). They include future *Pour le Mérite* recipient Oberleutnant Oskar Freiherr von Boenigk, then with Jasta 4 (fifth from left), and Leutnant der Reserve Egon Koepsch also of Jasta 4 (fifth

nant Franz Müller; Oberleutnant Karl Bodenschatz; Leutnant Hans Joachim Wolff; Leutnant der Reserve Alfred Niederhoff. Front row: Leutnant der Reserve Konstantin Krefft; Leutnant der Reserve Otto Brauneck; Leutnant der Reserve Wilhelm Bockelmann; Kurt Wolff; visiting artist Professor Arnold Busch;

from right). Döring had only three victories to his credit when he assumed temporary command of JG I, but he was a graduate of the Prussian Cadet Corps, a career officer and had command experience. He performed well, given the delicate task of having to report to Richthofen and to 4. Armee's Officer in

Charge of Aviation, Hauptmann Otto Bufe, who had his own ideas about how the Geschwader should operate (see Appendix I).

Right: Frustrated by hospital confinement, Richthofen pestered his superiors until on 25 July he was returned to command of JG I. Here, still looking peaky, he enjoys the sunlight on the steps at Château de Béthune with Geschwader officers, top row from left: Leutnant der Reserve Kurt Küppers from Jasta 6; Leutnant Carl August von Schoenebeck, Jasta 11; Oberleutnant Karl Scheffer, Jasta 11; Leutnant Wilhelm Bockelmann, Jasta 11; Oberleutnant Hans-Helmuth von Boddien, Jasta 11; Leutnant der Reserve Alfred Niederhoff, Jasta 11; Leutnant Justus Grassmann, Jasta 10. Front row from left: Leutnant der Reserve Konstantin Krefft, JG I; Richthofen; Leutnant Eberhard Mohnike, Jasta 11; Leutnant der Reserve Erwin Böhme, who succeeded Kurt Wolff as leader of Jasta 29. Geschwader Adjutant Bodenschatz wrote: 'St. Nicholas Hospital in Courtrai is not quite to be compared with a sanatorium. Peaceful silence is out of the question. During the day, troop columns clatter through the small city and night after night the heavy bombs of British squadrons thunder down on to the important communications centre. Freiherr von Richthofen and Leutnant Wolff do not worry about these bombs. Rather, they have worried thoughts about the Geschwader. Every day the Adjutant comes rushing in and brings the reports.'[7] The broken 'souvenir' from a British R.E.8 reconnaissance aeroplane had ironic significance, as Manfred von Richthofen's first grave marker was made from an R.E. propeller.

Left: On 30 July Richthofen welcomed former Jasta 2 comrade Leutnant Werner Voss (left) to JG I. Karl Bodenschatz recalled that although Voss was only 20 years old, 'with him, an "ace" has once again arrived: very young, wiry, 34 victories behind him, [and a recipient of] the *Orden Pour le Mérite*.'[8] He succeeded Oberleutnant Ernst Freiherr von Althaus, who had not lived up to his early promise as a

staff confirmed that his wounds were completely healed. Moreover, Wolff had been succeeded in command of Jasta 11 by Oberleutnant Wilhelm Reinhard and could not resume Staffel leadership until he was qualified to fly in combat. Here, Wolff manages a half smile while talking to (from left) JG I technical officer Konstantin Krefft, aeroplane designer and manufacturer Anthony Fokker and Geschwader Kommandeur von Richthofen.

Jagdstaffel leader and was transferred to instructor duties. In fact, Althaus was going blind, which kept him from performing as he had at the beginning of his career, when he became the eighth fighter pilot to receive the *Pour le Mérite*. At this time Voss was the second highest-scoring German fighter pilot and, with his bold fighting style, he was a strong contender to surpass Richthofen as his nation's most successful ace. Even though Richthofen was under strict orders not to resume combat flying, he embraced the challenge and, for the moment, seemed content to let the younger man add to his score.

Below: Having had to replace Freiherr von Althaus and keep Kurt Wolff from combat flying, Richthofen was given a lighter task following the announcement that Oberleutnant Eduard Dostler was to receive the *Pour le Mérite*. When he visited Jasta 6's mess to congratulate the Staffel leader, Richthofen placed his own *Pour le Mérite* around the 21-victory ace's neck, as seen here. Very likely, Dostler was allowed to wear Richthofen's award until his own arrived from the Orders Chancery in Berlin. The popular image of such events turning into great drinking bouts did not

Above: Leutnant Kurt Wolff (second from right) was released from hospital on 7 August and was eager to return to combat. Having already shot down 33 aeroplanes, he wanted to keep up with Werner Voss, whose 35th 'kill' on 10 August marked the beginning of a series of victories at the rate of several per week. Like Richthofen, however, Wolff was forbidden to fly in combat until the medical

south-west of Houthulst Forest and went right into the ground … '[10] The Nieuport was confirmed as his 58th victory, but the numerical strength of his Flight was reported differently by a British participant, Second Lieutenant James D. Payne: 'While on ground patrol with 2/Lt [William] H. T. Williams, we were attacked by eight Albatros scouts. The leader of the enemy formation dived on 2/Lt Williams, followed by the remainder. I turned and fired on the enemy leader, but after firing about five rounds, my gun jambed [sic]. I last saw 2/Lt Williams at about 600 feet still going down, under control, with some of the E.A. [enemy aircraft] formation on his tail.'[11]

hold true when Richthofen was involved, as former JG I pilot Hans-Georg von der Osten recalled: 'it was very rarely that we did any drinking in Jasta 11, as we always had to keep ourselves ready for action. This was not true for … Jasta 4, for instance, under Oberleutnant von Döring, [where] they sometimes had some very "wet" evenings.'[9]

Above: Richthofen returned to combat flying on 16 August 1917. He led the morning patrol and shot down a British Nieuport, like the one seen here. His combat report showed that convalescence had not dulled his airfighting skill: 'At about 7.55 a.m., accompanied by four aeroplanes of Staffel 11, I went after a small flight of Nieuports. After a long chase, I attacked an opponent and after a short fight I shot up his engine and fuel tank. The aeroplane went into a spin, [and] I followed right after it until just above the ground, [and] gave it one more shot, so that the aeroplane crashed

Below: Jagdgeschwader I had three other victories to celebrate that day – among them Werner Voss' 37th – but Manfred von Richthofen was unable to join the festivities. Drained by the day's combat, he went to bed early. He suffered from pounding headaches, aggravated by the thick bandage, conspicuous here (arrow), which he had to wear beneath his flying helmet. The next day, JG I added four more victories to its score,

including a special honour attendant on the first combat success of Leutnant Hans-Georg von der Osten. This pilot, Silesian born and, like his Kommandeur, a former Uhlan, recalled: 'On the evening of the same 17 August, Rittmeister von Richthofen suddenly ordered a bottle of champagne and announced that this, my first victory, had been the 200th victory of Jasta 11.'[12] Next morning the Commanding General of the Air Force sent a telegram: 'On 17 August, Jasta 11 defeated its 200th opponent in aerial combat since 12 October 1916, the day it was first mobilised. These successes are a shining example for all fighter pilots, [and] the finest memorial for the fallen comrades of Jasta 11. To the Jasta and its leader, Leutnant Wolff, and especially to its former leader, Rittmeister Freiherr von Richthofen, I express my appreciation.'[13]

Below: General der Infanterie Erich von Ludendorff (arrowed) and members of his staff accompanied Richthofen (to the General's left) during an inspection of Jagdstaffel 11 on Sunday, 19 August 1917.

Nominally the Quartermaster-General of the German Army, von Ludendorff functioned as Deputy Chief of Staff to Generalfeldmarschall Paul von Beneckendorf und von Hindenburg and, in fact, controlled the army during the war's last two years.[14] As JG I's war diary showed, however, Ludendorff was uninformed about the state of airfighting equipment: 'General Ludendorff comes to visit, to see for himself the most audacious pilots of the German Army and to shake their hands. On this occasion he can also see the newly arrived Triplanes, which every fighter pilot waits for longingly and which make an excellent impression.'[15] In fact, the new Fokker fighter which Richthofen had been promised were still on order while he was still convalescing and did not arrive until after Ludendorff's departure.[16] Accordingly, the example of the latest fighter in use was Richthofen's all-red Albatros D.V 2059/17, parked in the background with a ladder against the fuselage for any rear-area types who wanted to peer into the Kommandeur's 'office'.

Right: Next day, JG I provided air cover over Courtrai for Kaiser Wilhelm's inspection of various 4. Armee troops.[17] Richthofen, third from left, stands at ease in a relaxed moment prior to the monarch's arrival. He is wearing a wide bar of ribbons for awards he had received up to that point, surmounted by his *Pour le Mérite*, which he was rarely without. His slightly larger hat accommodated the bandage round his head. Hauptmann Paul Freiherr von Pechmann, to Richthofen's left, had flown 400 combat missions and

become the first observer to receive the *Pour le Mérite*.[18] Next in line is Oberleutnant Eduard Dostler, the 26-victory ace and leader of Jasta 6; a day later he was killed in combat with a two-seat reconnaissance aeroplane. A British report described the encounter on 21 August as the classic battle between a fighter pilot interdicting an enemy intelligence-gathering mission and a vigorous defence by a reconnaissance crew: 'When taking photographs, Lieut. [Norman] Sharples and 2nd-Lieut. M. O'Callaghan, No. 7 Squadron, were attacked by four Albatros Scouts. The observer opened fire at the nearest one, and it burst into flames and crashed. The other three E.A. were driven off by SPADs of No. 19 Squadron, which had arrived on the scene.'[19]

Right: As the Prussian monarch approaches the line of aviation personnel at Courtrai, Manfred von Richthofen steps forward and salutes him. General der Infanterie Friedrich Sixt von Armin, 65-year-old Commanding General of 4. Armee (right), had a motto consistent with Richthofen's own philosophy: 'He who does not dare to take the next step has made the whole journey for nothing.'[20]

Right: After the Kaiser's visit, Richthofen probably needed the comfort of his faithful Danish hound, Moritz. Next day, Hauptmann Helmuth Wilberg, 4. Armee's new Officer in Charge of Aviation, reminded the Kommandeur of the delicate state of his health. In a routine report Wilberg added a note that instructed Richthofen not to fly in combat unless it were absolutely necessary, and essentially grounded him in precise bureaucratic terms: 'I refer to the Army Order of 12 August, sub-paragraph II, and, if necessary, request notification in case this point is not being sufficiently taken into account.'[21]

Surely, Moritz was a reminder of happier, more care-free days, as Richthofen recalled: 'He slept in bed with me and was very well trained ... I even took him up with me once. He became my first 'observer'. He behaved himself very sensibly and eyed the world with interest from above. Only my mechanics grumbled later, as they had to clean the aeroplane of some unpleasant things. But Moritz was very pleased with it all.'

Below: An early-morning raid on JG I facilities by the RFC on 26 August was enough justification for Richthofen to ignore the irksome 'sub-paragraph II' and go after the attackers. SPAD S.7 fighters from No. 19 Squadron, RFC, like the one seen here, had struck airfields at Heule, Bisseghem and Marcke at about 0645 hours (German Time) and within an hour Richthofen led four Albatroses against a SPAD from the same unit and brought it down. He was credited with his 59th victory.[22] Two days later his letter home acknowledged that he was not totally fit for combat, but then he ignored his own warning: 'I am very happy about the state of Lothar's health. Under no circumstances should he be allowed at the Front until he has [regained] his full physical strength. Otherwise, he will have a relapse immediately or be shot down. I notice that I am not quite right myself. I have ... made two combat flights [within ten days]

and of course both were successful, but after each one I was completely exhausted. During my first one something bad almost happened to me. My wound is healing frightfully slow; it is still almost as big as a five-Mark piece. Yesterday, they removed yet another piece of bone; I believe it will be the last.'[23]

Above: The lack of reaction – or repercussion – following Richthofen's latest victory emboldened him to take a more active role in JG I operations. When the Geschwader's first Fokker Triplane arrived, on 28 August,[24] Jasta 10 leader Werner Voss made the preliminary flight checks, but Richthofen knew that he himself would soon be flying the aeroplane in battle. Three days later a formal demonstration of the Fokker F.I 102/17 was held at Marke and Richthofen was an eager participant. As seen here, he explained the fighter's combat features to Generalmajor Karl von Lossberg, 4. Armee's Chief of Staff. For Lossberg, who had been promoted to general officer rank just four weeks earlier,[25] this visit was a pleasant diversion after recent heavy fighting in the Third Battle of Ypres. For Richthofen, the Triplane promised what he sought in a fighter. He told his

men that he had been assured by his contacts at the Fokker factory in Schwerin that the Triplanes 'climb like monkeys and are as manoeuvrable as the devil'.[26]

Opposite page, top: A special guest at the Fokker Triplane demonstration was the new German Chancellor, Dr. Georg Michaelis (second from left). Having been in office for only seven weeks,[27] the head of the Reichstag (national parliament) was on his first visit to the Front and seemed pleased to have the demonstration explained by fellow Silesian Manfred von Richthofen. For this occasion, Richthofen wore the smallest possible bandage, above and behind his left ear. Even though Michaelis had no military background, the 59-year-old former civil servant wore the ribbon of the Iron Cross 2nd Class in a button hole on his tunic. His greatest contribution to the war effort at that point had been to persuade the Reichstag to approve 15 billion Reichsmarks (£734.25 million or US $3.75 billion) in war credits to pay for such equipment as the new Fokker Triplanes.[28]

Opposite page, centre: Next morning – 1 September 1917 – Richthofen made an even more important

demonstration in the new Fokker Triplane (seen here with Anthony Fokker in the pilot's seat), when he shot down a two-seater that was ranging British artillery east of Ypres. Richthofen reported: 'Flying the Triplane for the first time [in combat], I and four gentlemen of Staffel 11 attacked a courageously flown British artillery-spotter. I approached [until] it was 50 metres below me and fired 20 shots, whereupon the adversary went down out of control and crashed on this side [of the lines] near Zonnebeke.'[29] If Richthofen's 60th seemed too easy, there was an explanation which he was quick to recognise: 'Apparently the adversary had taken me for a British [Sopwith] triplane, as the observer stood up in his machine without making a move to attack me with his machine-gun.'[30]

Lower left: Manfred's self-satisfied grin while examining the wreckage of Sopwith Pup B.1795, his 61st victory, is understandable. Once again his new Fokker Triplane had performed well and, in this instance, against a spirited opponent, as he indicated in his combat report: 'With five aeroplanes of Staffel 11 involved in a fight with a formation of Sopwith single-seaters, I attacked an opponent at 3,500 metres and after a rather long aerial combat forced him to land near Bousbecque. I had the absolute conviction that I had before me a very skilful pilot, who at 50 metres' altitude still did not give up, [but] continued to fire and, even when flattening out [before landing], opened fire on an infantry column, then deliberately ran his machine into a tree. The Fokker Triplane F.I 102/17 is absolutely superior to the British Sopwith.'[31] Leutnant Eberhard Mohnike, seen lighting a cigarette behind Richthofen, also shot down a Sopwith Pup from the same flight and was credited with his sixth victory.[32]

Below: Richthofen's 61st opponent – Lieutenant Algernon F. Bird of No. 46 Squadron, RFC (right) – also managed a smile. He was one of 29 airmen who survived an encounter with Richthofen; another 54 are known to have been killed. The 21-year-old Norfolk man was doubly lucky because Richthofen's Flight was part of a larger formation which attacked the six Sopwith Pups that morning. The terse language of a British report could not mask the desperate situation of the Royal Flying Corps pilots: 'About 6.30 a.m., 20 Albatros ... [scouts were] encountered near Gheluwe and ... [we dived] on several over Wervicq. Lt. Wilcox engaged two E.A. and fired a couple of

bursts, but had to desist owing to attack from behind. Fighting ensued for about 20 minutes. Got separated, so returned. Lt [G. E.] Thompson dived on same lot, but four got on tail of [his] Sopwith and [he] had to desist. Fighting for 20 minutes [and] eventually recrossed line at 1,000 feet followed by two E.A. until line was reached. Lt [R. S.] Asher had a forced landing owing to engine failure, which prevented much assistance in fighting. Lt. McDonald and Lt. Bird [have] not returned.'[33] Lieutenant Kenneth W. McDonald died of his wounds next day.

Right: Richthofen was pleased when Fokker D.V biplanes, like the one behind him, arrived at JG I. These older aeroplanes were not intended for front-line use, but to provide experience with rotary engines, as most JG I pilots had flown only the stationary-engined Albatros and needed to understand the flight characteristics of the engines that would power their Fokker Triplanes. But before Richthofen logged much time in the fighter trainers

vaulted over it. By late summer 1917, however, the visit of a 60-victory fighter ace was no longer a private event. This time his mother, Kunigunde Freifrau von Richthofen, remembered: 'On the 17th of September, Manfred telegraphed that he would arrive by air that afternoon. We waited at the small parade ground [across the street from the house]. At six o'clock the [two-seat] red aeroplane that was now his private property appeared. In the last glow of a clear September day, it created the impression that it had burst forth from the sun. First,

or his new Triplane, the bureaucracy caught up with him. On 6 September, Geschwader Adjutant Bodenschatz recalled: 'Disregarding that sub-paragraph II of the Army Order of 12 August has rather strong consequences: the Rittmeister "voluntarily" begins a compulsory four-week leave which had been pushed vigorously by everyone in high places.'[34] Richthofen understood the purpose of the recuperative leave and made the most of it. When he was recognised by a fellow-passenger in a train en route to Berlin, he noted cheerfully: 'The Duke of Saxe–Coburg–Gotha invited me to hunt at his estate in Reinhardsbrunn and now I am going to meet Lothar in Berlin to just take it easy ... Do you know Berlin? Yes? Splendid! Then you must show us a bit of Berlin, as we really do not know it and, besides, we have no relatives there.'[35] The passenger had to decline the offer and, when the train arrived in the German capital, Richthofen soon blended into the crowd.

Right: The wrought-iron gate in front of the Richthofen house in Schweidnitz (now Swidnica, Poland) was no barrier to the agile Richthofen. Finding it locked on previous leaves, he had simply

Manfred flew over the city, where he was spotted and greeted with great jubilation. In a flash, the previously empty landing area was filled with people. The aeroplane set down as gently as a butterfly. Despite the cordons set up, we had trouble getting back to our house.'[36]

Below: Richthofen wore all his medals for what would be the last family portrait. With him were, standing from left: his mother, brothers Lothar and Bolko and his sister Ilse. His father, Major Albrecht Freiherr von Richthofen, was seated. Later, his mother wrote: 'This was the first time since Christmas 1915 that we all gathered together here. I was happy in the peace and security of my family.'[37] A few days later, however, when she asked Manfred about his wound, the conversation took a dark, almost foreshadowing tone: 'One after the other the magnificent young flying heroes had fallen. They had all been experts and showed unparalleled bravery. Now Manfred had tempted Fate – and been wounded. "How did it happen?" I asked him. "They really hit me," was the snappy answer. He knew where the shot had come from, but did not want to

say. Probably from the ground. We went through the garden and now I wanted to say what was on my mind: "Give up flying, Manfred." [He replied:] "Who would fight the war if we all thought that way? Only the soldier in the trenches? When the professional fails at leadership, soon it will be here as it is in Russia ... Would it please you if I were in some safe place and resting on my laurels?" No – there was nothing else to do; Manfred would fight on until – until – the war ended.'[38]

Right: Manfred is so often portrayed as the bold air warrior, steady in the face of any danger, that it is unusual to find him in the shy pose seen in this popular postcard. Could he have been mellowed by his mother's admonition? Or was it that, having learned of the death in combat of his protégé Kurt Wolff on 15 September and that of his rival, Werner Voss, eight days later, the fact of his own frail mortality was finally borne in upon him? In fact, neither was the case. The postcard had been contrived by superimposing a photograph of him in a relaxed setting far from the battlefront against a background featuring a crashed enemy aeroplane.

Right: The original photograph had appeared in a contemporary newspaper and showed Richthofen at a popular horse racing event in the Grunewald district of Berlin, and his demeanour merely betrayed his reticence in the company of women. While on leave he spent time with Erich von Salzmann, who clarified: 'Richthofen was with ladies repeatedly at my home in Berlin ... [and he showed] the flawless manner, the naturalness that women liked so much. He was not a ladies' man in the well-known sense of the word. He was anything but that. He was almost

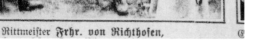

the personification of modern manliness, [and] the ladies liked him, even though he did not court them in every way as did many of the young cavaliers who had become famous. Once we were together at the races in Grunewald and for awhile he remained unnoticed. That morning he had been at Johannisthal, had test flown some new aeroplanes and his "dress" was not really very elegant racecourse attire. In general, Richthofen was little inclined towards superficial appearances, although he did not seek to neglect the way he looked. Suddenly people recognised him. Then the photographers came. I have seen other young celebrities in such moments, as they put on airs and posed. None of that for Richthofen. His complete self-assurance was obvious.'[39]

Below: A popular photograph of Richthofen and Käte Otersdorf, his nurse at the hospital in Courtrai, might have suggested a romantic link, but the rigid pose of both and the distance between them clearly signalled that theirs was an entirely professional rela-

tionship. American journalist Floyd Gibbons recorded that Richthofen received many letters from adoring women throughout Germany, but, unfortunately, they have been lost to history. Also missing is correspondence from a young woman who was said to have attracted his special attention. Kunigunde Freifrau von Richthofen told Gibbons: 'Manfred loved this one girl. He had for her the love of an honourable man for the woman he wanted to be the mother of his children. I know that she loved him.'[40]

Below: In a more candid setting, such as this photograph taken in May 1917, when Richthofen and his friend Fritz Falkenhayn flew to Bad Homburg for a visit to Kaiserin Auguste Viktoria, Richthofen's shyness with women is more apparent. While Falkenhayn mixes easily with members of the imperial entourage – in this case the Forckenbeck-Gablenz sisters – Richthofen virtually retreated behind the aeroplane.

Right: When Richthofen (fifth from left) finally attended a wedding, it was that of his friend and former Kampfgeschwader 2 comrade Hauptmann Fritz Prestien (arrowed) on 18 October 1917. The event was held at Reinhardsbrunn Castle in Gotha, the bride's father being chief estate manager at the Court of Saxe–Coburg–Gotha and its reigning duke, who had befriended Richthofen early in his career. Among the notables at the festivities were, from left: Wolf Freiherr Pergler von Perglas and his wife; Gerda von Minckwitz and Oberjägermeister Major a.D. Hans von Minckwitz (parents of the bride); Richthofen, in full medals and wearing a Uhlan's *Tschapka* dress helmet; Duchess Viktoria Adelheid and Duke Carl Eduard of Saxe–Coburg–Gotha; three Court officials; Wally von Minckwitz and Fritz Prestien (the bridal pair); various court, military and family members. That evening when Richthofen returned to his room at the Continental Hotel in Berlin, he was roundly congratulated. He learned that the German press had misunderstood the

story and reported that *he* had married Wally von Minckwitz. Likewise telegrams and congratulatory messages were sent to his father at his military post and his mother back in Schweidnitz.[41] It took a few days for the error to be corrected.

Right: The photograph of Manfred in a nun's habit was obtained later for display in the Richthofen Museum at Schweidnitz. The story behind it appeared in a later edition of his memoirs: 'A young lady who said she came from a good family wrote to me. This lady is a novice and will become a nun. In her convent cell she has a picture of me that she had picked up somewhere. And then one day something bad happened: the abbess came into the cell and saw the picture. The novice received a severe reprimand and was told that prospective nuns should not have pictures of men hanging in their cells – not even when these men are well-known fighter pilots. The novice, therefore, had to remove the picture. But ... she did something that perhaps flatters if not misrepresents me. She wrote to a friend who was already a nun and asked her to send a large photograph of herself. The friend did that. Then the poor girl cut

out the face of the photograph and stuck my face under the nun's habit.'[42]

6 — A Flyer Through and Through

Below: The area then occupied by 4. Armee included facilities used by German bomber and ground-support fighters which Jagdgeschwader I had to escort to their targets. Manfred von Richthofen did not want such restrictions placed on his pilots; he preferred to let them range far and wide to shoot down the British counterparts of the air units he had to protect. He followed orders, of course, and JG I units flew escort missions. In conjunction with this unpleasant duty, Richthofen flew to the large bomber base at Gontrode – south-east of Ghent in Belgium – to confer with Hauptmann Rudolf Kleine (left), commander of Kampfgeschwader 3, and his adjutant, Oberleutnant Gerlich (centre). Earlier, Kleine had served in Kampfgeschwader 1, the successor to the

Brieftauben-Abteilung at Ostend, which gave him and Richthofen mutual interests. The KG 3 leader was Richthofen's peer in all respects: he was a Geschwader-Kommandeur and had been awarded the *Orden Pour le Mérite*. But the fighter escorts were of little use to Kleine when, during a night raid on 14 December 1917, his bomber was shot down by British A.A. fire.[1]

Opposite page, bottom: Adding to the confusion of just how 'red' Richthofen's aeroplane was, is this companion view to the preceding photograph, taken during his visit to KG 3. The pale white Gotha G.IV bombers inside the old Zeppelin hangar at the left contrast starkly with the dark Albatros D.Vs in

photographs of Albatros D.V 2059/17, in which he scored his 58th and 59th victories. JG I pilots continued to fly the Albatros after the Fokker Triplanes arrived in strength and, later, when problems with the Triplanes occurred.

Left: Manfred von Richthofen and Werner Voss had flown Fokker F.I Triplane V 4 prototypes in combat. The first Fokker Dr.I production model to reach the Front – 115/17 seen here – did not go to JG I, but was assigned to Leutnant Heinrich Gontermann, leader of Jagdstaffel 15, on 7. Armee's front. When Richthofen

which Richthofen and another pilot – very probably Leutnant der Reserve Konstantin Krefft, JG I's technical officer – flew to Gontrode. All national markings on the Albatros in the foreground have been overpainted and this one may also have been used by Richthofen. The other aeroplane matches returned to JG I on 23 October, he flew Fokker Dr.I 114/17. Within a week, however, a series of Triplane losses occurred. On 29 October, Jasta 11 pilot Vizefeldwebel Josef Lautenschlager was killed while flying Dr.I 113/17; an official report stated candidly that it 'had been shot down by one of our own flyers'[2]

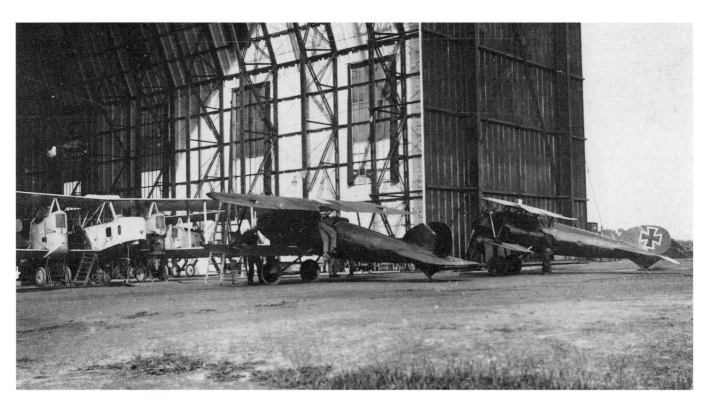

having been mistaken for a Sopwith Triplane. The following day, the Richthofen brothers were on their first flight together in more than five months when Lothar had to land his Triplane. Manfred followed him down and, on landing, his Dr.I 114/17 began to fall apart.[3] He was unhurt but the aeroplane was written off. Less fortunate was Gontermann, a 39-victory ace and *Pour le Mérite* recipient, who lost

ribs from the top wing spar of Dr.I 115/17 while he was flying over his own airfield; the Triplane crashed and later that day he died of his injuries.[4] On 31 October, Leutnant der Reserve Günther Pastor of Jasta 11 was on a routine flight in Dr.I 121/17 when it broke up in mid-air and he fell to his death.[5]

Above right: On 2 November all Fokker Triplanes were grounded while the recent structural failures were investigated. Richthofen (second from left, saluting) returned to flying Albatros D.V 4693/17, in which he had been forced down on 6 July. The Albatros seen here seems to be D.V 4693/17 (see page 74), except for the national marking on the vertical stabiliser, which may have been applied during repairs while its pilot was in hospital. Later that month the Geschwader moved to the Avesnes-le-Sec area, north-east of Cambrai, on 2. Armee's front, and Richthofen was flying D.V 4693/17 when he gained his 62nd victory. He was leading Flights from JG I and Jagdstaffeln 5 and 15 over Bourlon Wood, where British and Australian fighters were supporting their ground troops' advance against Cambrai. German pilots were credited with shooting down five British aeroplanes that day, including an Airco D.H.5 confirmed for Manfred von Richthofen, and his brother Lothar's 26th victory, a Bristol F.2B.[6] British records show greater losses that day, but most Royal Flying Corps pilots

involved returned to their own lines and many damaged machines were described as 'unsalvageable', rather than as combat losses.[7]

Above: An original of this photograph of the wreckage of an Airco D.H.5 in the markings of No. 64 Squadron, RFC, was displayed in the Richthofen Museum in Schweidnitz. It may show one of two

Left: The onset of winter can be seen as Manfred (left) and Lothar von Richthofen (second from right), who had been leader of Jagdstaffel 11 since 24 September, walked across the sparse landscape of their new airfield. Jasta 11 member Hans-Georg von der Osten noted the change in weather and living accommodation when he returned 'just in time for the transfer of the Geschwader to the vicinity of Cambrai to support the battle for Bourlon Wood. We were quartered in Avesnes-le-Sec, not in a castle, but in the village and our mess was in [a local] inn. Bourlon Wood was soon transformed into a heap of shell-torn ground. On these numerous flights under Manfred ... or Lothar, we had many a fight in the air. During November and December I often flew with Manfred ... [but] actually he was always on his own. When we flew in a group someone was always ordered to stay near him ... Once during the winter I had a frozen nose. We had face masks, but the nose stuck out. Our flying-suits were shapeless and crudely made. I think the British [suits] were tailored better. For myself, I did all my flying in a leather suit, trousers and a leather jacket and, beneath that, a heavy pullover.'[10]

D.H.5s that Manfred von Richthofen engaged on 23 November 1917. Even though the RFC machine credited to Richthofen – A.9299 – came down within British lines, the German ace received a patch of fabric bearing its serial number and sent it home for his growing souvenir collection. After forcing down one D.H.5 west of Bourlon Wood, Richthofen shot down a second, piloted by 22-year-old Lieutenant James A. V. Boddy, who crashed in the south-east corner of the wood. Royal Air Force Historian H. A. Jones recorded: 'Another D.H.5 pilot ... while firing on German troops in retreat from the wood, was brought down ahead of the British infantry, by a direct hit on his aeroplane from a shell. When he had extricated himself from the wreckage he saw Lieutenant Boddy's aeroplane crashing into the trees; he went across and rescued the pilot and the two made their way safely to a British dressing-station.'[8] The second pilot was No. 64 Squadron's Captain Henry R. Fox Russell, who was awarded the Military Cross for rescuing Boddy.[9]

Below: Leutnant der Reserve Hans Klein (right), the leader of Jasta 10, was crowned with success on 30 November 1917. Just after noon he shot down a British observation balloon west of Cambrai for his

22nd victory and later that day he was informed by telegram that the Kaiser had conferred upon him the *Pour le Mérite*. That afternoon JG I was back over Bourlon Wood and, as Manfred von Richthofen later reported about his 63rd success: 'With Leutnant [Lothar] von Richthofen and Leutnant [der Reserve Siegfried] Gussmann, at 2.30 p.m. we attacked an enemy single-seat formation of ten Englishmen just over the front-line positions. After I had fired at various Englishmen, I came into close firing range behind a single-seater, which after 100 shots fell burning in the area of the small wooded quarry'[11] near Moeuvres. But it was not an altogether rosy day, as Hans-Georg von der Osten learned: ' ... with the cloud ceiling at only 400 metres, I managed to shoot down a D.H.5 out of a group which had suddenly appeared out of the clouds above. It crashed into the shell-torn ground south of Bourlon Wood. Immediately after [my] landing, Richthofen congratulated me, but at the same time rebuked me because after my first attack I had not followed the crippled aeroplane into the first turn. I had had to turn away because of the attack by another Englishman who, as we used to say in front-line German, "was spitting into my crate from behind". I mention this to show how closely Richthofen kept watch over the entire battle scene.'[12]

Below: Despite increasingly bad weather, Richthofen – seen here prior to take-off from Moorsele, Belgium – flew continually, often working with newly arriving pilots. The reaction of Leutnant Friedrich-Wilhelm Lübbert, who joined Jasta 11 in early December, was typical of the men in whom the Kommandeur took an interest: 'Richthofen was a flyer through and through. Over time he became one of the most popular men in Germany. One would think that a man who was so preoccupied with one of the most strenuous activities there is and who enjoyed the great popularity he did would have no room within himself for friendship and comradeship. The opposite was the case. Richthofen was just as good a comrade as he was a superior officer for the officers of his Staffel and his Geschwader. He associated with us off duty as any other comrade [would] ... One could go to him with any question and any trouble, and find sympathy and help when they were needed.'[13]

Right: Appearing in a postcard photograph with Richthofen was a great honour for a fighter pilot. This photograph taken at Avesnes-le-Sec in early 1918 was not selected – a different view of the group became Sanke Postcard No. 606 – but offers another glimpse of the young eagles who would fight during the coming spring offensive. They are from left: Feldwebelleutnant Friedrich Schubert; Leutnant der Reserve Siegfried Gussmann; Leutnant Werner Steinhäuser; Leutnant Hans Karl von Linsingen; Leutnant Karl Esser; Leutnant Hans-Georg von der Osten; Leutnant Eberhard Mohnike; Leutnant Friedrich-

Wilhelm Lübbert; Oberleutnant Hans-Helmuth von Boddien; Vizefeldwebel Edgar Scholz. Except for Schubert, who was assigned to Jasta 6, all the others are from Jasta 11. Service under Richthofen was not easy, as Lübbert observed: 'Every young pilot who came to his Staffel had to fly a few times at the Front alone. After the flight the details of what the beginner had seen and experienced were discussed thoroughly. Richthofen ... kept in the Staffel only pilots who really accomplished something ... [If] he became convinced that the person concerned was not up to the requirements that [he] placed on a fighter pilot – whether due to his moral character or due to his technical ability – that person would surely be sent away.'[14]

Lower left: While the problems besetting Fokker Triplanes were being investigated by an Air Force commission, other manufacturers sought to fill the gap in first-line fighter coverage and to enlarge their own government contracts. On 12 December, when Richthofen reported to the Pfalz Flugzeugwerke (Aeroplane Works) at Speyer am Rhein to test fly the firm's triplane prototype, company founder and co-owner Alfred Everbusch leaned over the rear of the aeroplane and offered comments. At that time the German Palatinate was part of the Kingdom of Bavaria which had its own aviation administration and production facilities. Richthofen was entirely candid about the proposed successor to the Fokker Triplane: the supposedly more powerful Siemens-Halske Sh III geared rotary engine was a disappointment and the Pfalz Dr.I did not handle as well as the Fokker Dr.I he had flown at the Front. From the uneasy look he gave the photog-

rapher, Richthofen may have realised that he would have to 'make do' with the Albatros D.V and Pfalz D.III fighters then in JG I's inventory.

Below: Richthofen's status as a popular postcard figure helped the Geschwader even when he was away from the Front. Oberleutnant (later General der Flieger) Karl Bodenschatz, who published a personalised and expanded version of the JG I war diary in 1935, noted in his third-person narrative how the Kommandeur's image kept the Geschwader well-provisioned in otherwise lean times: 'The Adjutant sets out to undertake some little journeys to secure provisions and perhaps to lay hands on something special somewhere. There is, of course, scarcely anything to be had in the broad area, not for love nor money. Until one day he chances upon a marvellous remedy. And, from then on, whenever he comes across someone who has all manner of good things to offer, but who shrugs his shoulders and

regretfully spreads out his hands, then the Adjutant reaches into his coat pocket and pulls out a postcard. On this postcard is depicted Rittmeister von Richthofen, in his finest uniform with all his decorations and with his most winsome face (see page 10) and, moreover, at the bottom of the photograph is his signature written in his own hand. And that [device] works wonders and proves to be more precious and valuable and more effective than love or money. The Adjutant no longer comes back from his little journeys empty-handed.'[15]

Below: Winter weather curtailed flight operations on both sides of the lines. Manfred returned from the Pfalz factory on 20 December and, with the lull in activity, gladly welcomed his father to spend Christmas with Lothar and him at JG I. It was the last time the three men were together. The affection that JG I members had for them shows in comments by

Oberleutnant Wilhelm Reinhard, who was then leader of Jasta 6: 'Richthofen's father was generally known by everyone in the Geschwader as *"der Fliegervater"* [Father of the Flyers] and rightly so. His sons were indeed two flying heroes. The number of victories of both [eventually] reached the impressive level of 120. A third son [Karl Bolko] is still in the Cadet Institute in Wahlstatt. Father Richthofen also flew, of course not over the enemy [lines], but to visit his sons and not just once, but often. Such a visit was a day of honour for the Geschwader. When it was reported to our Kaiser, he was glad and said to those around him: "What, the Old Man flies, too?" Father Richthofen had, despite his age [58], placed himself at the service of the State; although, as he was hard of hearing, he could no longer fight in the front-line but became a garrison commander. It was a splendid sight when Father Richthofen spent time with us, flanked by his two sons.'[16]

Above: Fog, snow and then high winds reduced air activity during the Christmas season.[17] The relatively quiet time allowed for a photograph of Kommandeur von Richthofen and a gathering of new and old

Geschwader members, many of whom were his personal choices, as Adjutant Bodenschatz noted: 'The Rittmeister seeks out his own people. During the winter he drove around to Jasta schools and [other] Jagdstaffeln and watched their operations. He has long since stopped having his fighter pilots assigned "through official channels". He is allowed to fetch them himself. And if anyone has an eye for . . . those who can shoot and fly, for daredevils and non-daredevils, it is he.'[18] Seated from left: Leutnant der Reserve Karl Hertz, Jasta 4 (KiA 9 May); Leutnant der Reserve Robert Tüxen, Jasta 6; Oberleutnant Hans-Helmuth von Boddien, Jasta 11; Rittmeister Manfred von Richthofen, JG I (KiA 21 April); Leutnant der Reserve Hans Klein, Jasta 10; Oberleutnant Kurt-Bertram von Döring, Jasta 4; Oberleutnant Wilhelm Reinhard, Jasta 6 (KiC 3 July); Leutnant Lothar von Richthofen, Jasta 11; Leutnant der Reserve Konstantin Krefft, JG I. Standing from left: two unidentified pilots; Leutnant der Reserve Justus Grassmann, Jasta 10; unidentified; Leutnant der Reserve Max Kühn, Jasta 10; unidentified; Leutnant der Reserve Alois Heldmann, Jasta 10; Vizefeldwebel Adam Barth, Jasta 10 (KiA 30 January); unidentified.

Right: Manfred ended up in the murky background of a newspaper photograph during his and Lothar's visit to the German–Russian peace negotiations on 4 January 1918. The Commander-in-Chief of German Forces in the East, Prince Leopold of Bavaria (lower left), had invited many notable Germans to watch him humble the virtually defeated Russians. He had not counted on dealing with such tough Bolsheviks as Anastasia Bitsenko (third from right at the table), however, and, when V. I. Lenin's emissaries dragged out the talks for weeks, the Prince was unable to keep his gallery of notables at Brest-Litovsk. Richthofen described the lighter side of events: 'Meanwhile ... I had the opportunity to ... view all the commotion of the peace negotiations and to become personally acquainted with the gentlemen concerned. I almost had Frau Bitsenko as a [dinner] companion. It would have been a grand, amusing conversation. I would have enjoyed it, for she had also hunted down some of her enemies.

Although they were ministers and grand dukes and the like, whom she had banned to penal colonies in Siberia; nevertheless, there would have been a common point of conversation [for us].'[19]

Below: In mid-January Richthofen joined a distinguished group of fighter pilots at the aviation testing facility at Adlershof outside Berlin. From left are: Jagdstaffel 10 pilot Leutnant Erich Löwen-

hardt; Jasta 26 leader Oberleutnant Bruno Loerzer; Richthofen; Hauptmann Schwarzenberger, a staff officer; Leutnant der Reserve Hans Klein and another staff officer. The front-line pilots evaluated and compared a variety of new or improved fighters to help the Inspectorate of Aviation decide which to recommend for the coming year. Some 28 were offered, representing the best fighter designs from most of the leading companies: AEG, Albatros, Aviatik, Fokker, LFG Roland, Pfalz, Rumpler, Schütte-Lanz and Siemens-Schuckert. Away from the excitement at the airfield, the manufacturers offered refreshments and entertainment back in the German capital; Anthony Fokker hosted his guests at the exclusive Hotel Bristol, the Pfalz staff were set up in the Hotel Adlon, and other companies' representatives offered suitable hospitality at other fine hotels nearby.[20]

Right: Richthofen was rarely alone at official functions; he was followed by admirers or staff officers, attending to his needs. Even Anthony Fokker (seen here at left) joined the entourage. During the fighter trials, Richthofen managed to slip away and had one interesting experience, as Hans-Georg von der Osten related: 'On a rainy day we drove back from Adlershof to Berlin by car. On the way Richthofen said: "Well, I will get out here at Schulte's [art gallery] and have a look at the pictures Fritz Reusing has painted." Richthofen wore an overcoat with a big collar, typical of the officers' coats that we had before the war. As it was raining, [the coat] acted like a disguise. He went in [to the gallery] and came upon a painting that showed him in his aeroplane, captioned "Rittmeister Freiherr von Richthofen". An elderly gentleman came over and stood beside him. Richthofen said to him: "I beg your pardon but I am told that I have some likeness to this painting." The gentleman put on his spectacles, took a look at the picture, took a look at Richthofen,

and finally said: "I think you can forget that notion." Ten minutes later Richthofen joined us at the hotel, beaming with joy, and related the incident to us.'[21]

Below: The government commission investigating Fokker Triplane crashes concluded that shoddy workmanship was largely to blame. A contrite Fokker management promised improvements and the final production machines in the series began arriving at the Front in late December in preparation for the March 1918 offensive.[22] Further problems with the Albatros and even with the new Fokker Triplanes – Jasta 11's Leutnant Hans Joachim Wolff had experienced top-wing failure on 3 February[23] –

weighed on Richthofen's mind. And, adding to his list of things to think about, just before he returned to the Front, his brother developed a severe inflammation of the inner ear, which caused Manfred to write home: 'It is too bad that my duties in Berlin dragged on for so long that I could not come back to Schweidnitz once more ... Now I think I will not be able to come back to Germany for a long time. [Meanwhile,] Lothar should stay at home as long as possible; he is very careless with his ears and does nothing at all to take care of them. He is missing nothing here. I want him to know that he should not come back before the 1st of March. Should things start up strongly here, I will notify him by wire.'[24]

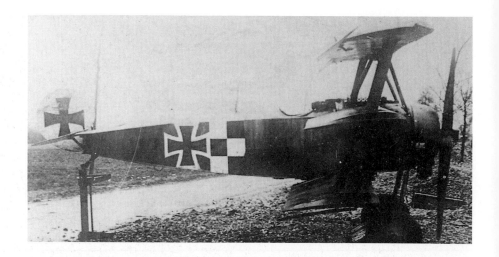

Above right: British intelligence specialists had their first look at an intact Fokker Triplane when this example – Dr.I 144/17 – came down within their lines on 13 January 1918. According to initial German reports, a Jagdstaffel 11 aeroplane was missing after attacking a British observation balloon near Heudi-court. A British account for that date stated: 'No. 41 Section's balloon was destroyed by an enemy triplane. The observers both made safe parachute descents. The triplane was brought down in our lines by A.A. fire, and is numbered G.125.'[25] Almost six weeks later,

JG I was informed: 'The Prisoner Information Bureau of the Württemberg Red Cross Society in Stuttgart has been notified by British Headquarters that Leutnant Eberhard Stapenhorst ... was taken prisoner near Cambrai on 13 January 1918 and, on 30 January 1918, was brought to England.'[26] Over the years, photographs of Fokker Dr.I 144/17 have appeared in print and have been mis-identified as a 'Red Baron' machine. The aeroplane was displayed in the Agricultural Hall in London for a time and then was discarded.[27]

Left: The Richthofen brothers strike a serious pose alongside a new Fokker Dr.I, which was still regarded with caution by German pilots. A British intelligence summary of 1 March 1918 accurately reported: 'Richthofen's squadron is being equipped with Fokker triplanes with a much improved aileron control.'[28] That same day, however, Jasta 11's Leutnant Eberhard Mohnike was wounded in action while flying Fokker Dr.I 155/17,[29] the same machine in which Hans Joachim Wolff had experienced structural problems four weeks earlier. Nagging doubts

about the Fokker Triplanes were compounded by other developments, as described by Lothar von Richthofen: 'Spring 1918 was [marked by] total ambush air operations on the part of the British. It was a bad time [for us] to score. The British artillery and ground-support aeroplanes, which had to fly lower, flew many kilometres over our side. Reconnaissance flights seldom came over to us and then only at tremendous altitudes, never below 5,000 metres. I had just come back to the Front after being treated for a middle ear inflammation and yearned to shoot down Englishmen. My brother was always in fine form.'[30]

Above: Manfred (centre) wore modest attire when he posed with the Staffel leaders who would face JG I's challenges during the spring offensive. In a plain tunic and without his *Pour le Mérite*, he is seen here with (from left): Leutnant der Reserve Kurt Wüsthoff, Jasta 4; Oberleutnant Wilhelm Reinhard, Jasta 6; Leutnant Erich Löwenhardt, Jasta 10; Leutnant Lothar von Richthofen, Jasta 11. Wüsthoff succeeded Leutnant der Reserve Hans Klein who had been wounded in action on 19 February and required a long convalescence. Wüsthoff was known to have a mercurial temperament, but was a very successful fighter pilot and Richthofen anticipated that the 21-year-old Rhinelander and *Pour le Mérite* recipient would inspire his subordinates to follow his example. The victor of 26 fights when he assumed command of Jasta 4, Wüsthoff shot down only one more enemy aeroplane before being transferred from the Staffel to the Geschwader staff. On 16 March he was succeeded by Leutnant Hans-Georg von der Osten, who recalled that Wüsthoff was 'very much younger than all his pilots and he had a very cheeky way. Apart from not being a very sympathetic man, he reported victories which he did not always check. So, Richthofen relieved him as Staffel leader.'[31]

Lower right: In March 1918, Lothar von Richthofen used his Fokker Triplane to good advantage, shooting down one Bristol F.2B on the 11th and two of the fast and manoeuvrable two-seat fighters on the 12th. His first encounter was against old adversaries, No. 48 Squadron, who fought fiercely. Lothar was credited with his 27th victory in this fight, but the F.2Bs also claimed success. Second Lieutenant Herbert H. Hartley encountered eight Fokker Dr.Is and four Pfalz D.IIIs, the latter probably from Jasta 10, and reported: 'I dived on one triplane, firing a burst of 50 rounds. The triplane spun [down] for about 1,000 feet, then fell on its back and went down quite out of control, zigzagging to and fro, often on its back. This is confirmed by the observer of Lt. Hilton's machine.'[32] No German triplane losses were recorded that day, but RFC records show that two F.2Bs were heavily damaged in that fight: A.7227 piloted by

Second Lieutenant W. L. Watson with Corporal J. Bowles as gunner and A.7114 flown by Lieutenant Hartley, whose observer/gunner, Lieutenant John H. Robertson, died of his wounds.[33] It is likely that one of the F.2Bs was Lothar's victim. Three days later, Hartley was killed by German ground fire.[34] He was 19 years old.

Right: Manfred von Richthofen flew Fokker Dr.I 152/17 on 12 March, when he led JG I against ten Bristol F.2Bs just south-east of the Geschwader's airfield. He reported: 'The aeroplane I attacked immediately dived down to 1,000 metres and tried to escape. The observer had fired only [when] high up in the air, [and] then disappeared in his seat and began shooting again only shortly before the machine landed. During the fight we drifted off to Le Catelet. There I forced my adversary to land and, after doing this, both crewmen left the aeroplane.'[35] Manfred was credited with his 64th victory. At about the same time, Lothar shot down two more aeroplanes, his 28th and 29th victories, and Leutnant Werner Steinhäuser got his fourth 'kill.'[36] Lieutenant Percy Hampton, a survivor of the battle, in which No. 62 Squadron lost four F.2Bs, recalled: 'It was really very similar to other large "dogfights" we had

aeroplane immediately burst into a large ball of flame and he and his observer, Lieutenant Gill, immediately jumped overboard, so I was able to report his certain death on my return.'[37]

Below: The crash of Lothar von Richthofen's Fokker Triplane is mute testimony to plans gone awry. While endeavouring to boost his score to 30

been having ... There were probably 25–30 [aeroplanes] engaged, so we had to look for other E.A. and [avoid] collisions. On that day ... Captain Kennedy [leader of "A" Flight] ... was abreast of me about 50 yards to starboard when [he was] hit. The

the following day, he was knocked down by Captains Geoffrey F. Hughes and Hugh Claye of the same Bristol F.2B unit whose losses had provided his most recent victories. One RFC report noted that this crew of No. 62 Squadron 'in a general engagement between

[their] patrol and a very large formation of E.A. scouts, shot down one E.A. triplane, which was confirmed by other members of the patrol to have crashed. [Captain Hughes] then attacked one of three triplanes which were diving on his tail. The E.A. went down vertically; the top plane was seen falling away in pieces. Capt. Hughes was then attacked by at least six other Albatros scouts and [Fokker] triplanes. The observer's gun was out of action and [Captain Claye] found it impossible to keep the E.A. off his tail, but he finally out-distanced all the E.A. except one Fokker triplane which was handled remarkably well. Capt. Hughes managed to eventually out-manoeuvre this machine with the engine full on and succeeded in recrossing the lines at 3,000 feet.'[38]

Below: Lothar von Richthofen, who spent the next four months in hospital, later wrote: 'I attacked my opponent in a dive. Then, there was a loud crack in my machine! It was hit. All too soon I realised what

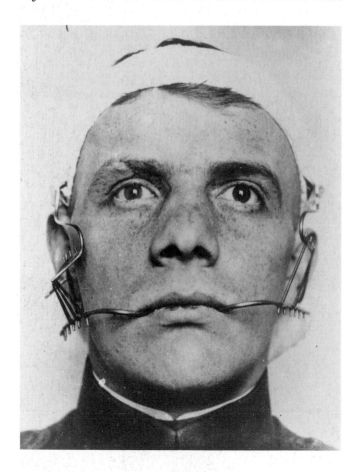

was wrong. I was flying a triplane ... [which] had suddenly become a biplane. It was a horrible feeling to be minus a wing at 4,000 metres. Post-haste, I broke away from my Englishman ... With the wings remaining I could still make a normal gliding flight, but only straight ahead, as the rudder was no longer functioning ... Before me lay a great clear space. I wanted to land there. While one could generally estimate in metres where to land the machine, this time I miscalculated. When I was at just 500 metres' altitude, suddenly I saw a high-tension wire before me. I could no longer go over it and I could not go under it, as two troop-columns were marching beneath it. I did not want to take other people with me to the hereafter. Therefore I had to make a turn. But that could no longer be done. Damn it all! [Now I find myself] lying in bed. Four sterile white walls! There is a nurse at my bedside, therefore I am in a hospital. My head is bandaged and I cannot touch it ... Now it dawns on me: I wanted to land and make a turn! In the attempt to turn, I crashed and lost consciousness.'[39]

Opposite page, top: After a call to JG I reported that Lothar had been killed, Manfred flew to the crash site at Arleux. Recognisable by his fur flying-coat, Manfred is seen here in an Albatros D.V at Jasta 5's airfield at Boistrancourt while seeking information about his brother. During the same late morning combat, Manfred shot down a Sopwith Camel, which was credited as his 65th triumph.[40] Captain Augustus H. Orlebar of No. 73 Squadron, who also claimed credit for Lothar's demise, witnessed Manfred's victory. He wrote in his combat report: 'While on Offensive Patrol, my formation encountered about 35 E.A., which were flying at heights varying from 17,000 to 10,000 ft. After diving at several groups of machines and engaging them, I eventually met an Albatros scout, into which I put several good bursts at close range. He turned over on his back and went down upside down. Afterwards, I dived on a Fokker triplane and opened fire at 100 yards' range. He instantly nose-dived and his top plane came off. I next saw two triplanes and two Albatros scouts attacking one Camel. I dived to help him, but both guns

jammed. However, I stunted around the E.A. as if attacking them and they all dived away.'[41]

Right: In preparation for thc Spring 1918 Offensive, Manfred von Richthofen was often underway in his staff car, as seen in a film clip. He wanted the most effective air combat team possible and a worthy successor to Lothar as leader of Jasta 11. Rain curtailed flight operations in mid-March, so Richthofen drove to Jasta 37's airfield, where 21-year-old Leutnant der Reserve Ernst Udet had built an impressive reputation (see Appendix I). Then a 20-victory ace and in line for the *Pour le Mérite*, Udet showed the tenacity and drive that Richthofen required. As always, the Kommandeur's presence and personal magnetism were powerful. 'I saluted him silently and looked at him,' Udet recalled. 'A calm, completely dominating face, [with] big, cold eyes, half-covered by heavy lids. This was the man who ... [was] the best of all of us.' Asked whether he was ready to join JG I, Udet responded with the usual brisk *'Jawohl, Herr Rittmeister'*. In fact, he was elated: 'Would I like to? Of course I would like

to. I would like it enormously. And if I had any say in the matter, I would have packed up immediately and gone back [to JG I] with him. There were many good Jagdstaffeln in our Armee and Jasta 37 was not the worst. But there was only one Jagdgeschwader Richthofen.'42

Above right: Under clear skies on 17 March, Richthofen borrowed this Jasta 6 machine – Fokker Dr.I 525/17 – to fly to Jasta 5's airfield at Boistrancourt, south-west of JG I's current location. Advance facilities for the coming offensive were being prepared for JG I at nearby Awoingt and, as his Geschwader would work closely with Jagdgruppe 2 (Jastas 5 and 46) once the battle began, Richthofen needed to have good liaison with his new neighbours. In any event, Jasta 5 was in no danger of having the talent-hungry Richthofen take away its leader, Hauptmann Richard Flashar. An old comrade of Richthofen's since their days together in Kampfstaffel 8, Flashar had scored only two victories since becoming Jasta 5's leader in July 1917. He had, however, done an outstanding job in leading his Staffel against British tanks during the Battle of Cambrai at the end of November 1917, and had mentored two *Pour le Mérite* winners, Leutnants Otto Könnecke and Fritz Rumey. Flashar had the spirit, if not the record, of success that Richthofen required.

Below: While others seemed awed by their guest, Jasta 5 leader Richard Flashar (second from right), retained his

composure. Like Richthofen, he knew the value of keeping a cool head. At one point during the Battle of Cambrai five months earlier, Flashar recalled that the 'telephone clanged without interruption: "Tanks at the Front, [enemy] flyers over the trenches!" Only calm blood [here]. Perhaps the weather will clear up in a short time so that take-off would be humanly possible. Now the Chief of Staff for the [2.] Armee high command is on the telephone, very agitated and nervous: "Why are you not flying?" I try to make him understand that at the moment it is

out of the question to go to the Front; right after take-off one will be in the midst of the thickest fog, gaining orientation is impossible, no aeroplane will find the front lines, the pilots will become disoriented and the machines of the Armee's only Jagdstaffel will be smashed during forced landings. My reasons are in no way acknowledged: British aeroplanes are over the Front, [and] I had better take off immediately. Yes, I was threatened with a court-martial! ... So, just to do something, I went out on a test flight by myself. As foreseen, it was completely useless! Half an hour later, it finally became a shade brighter.'[43]

Above: In a relaxed moment between flights, Manfred von Richthofen (fourth from right) chats with his subordinates. The captured British Nissen hut in the background was easily transportable and added to JG I's mobility and, thereby, to its success. Ernst Udet observed: 'Other Staffeln live in castles or small villages 20 or 30 kilometres behind the Front. The Richthofen Geschwader is crowded into corrugated metal huts that can be dismantled in a few hours and then re-assembled. They are seldom more than 20 kilometres behind the most advanced line. Other Staffeln take off two or three times a day, Richthofen and his people go up five times. Others

suspend flying in bad weather, [but] here we fly almost all the time.'[44]

Below: And fly the Geschwader did, late on the morning of 18 March. Thirty strong, and led by its Kommandeur, JG I ripped into a larger force of British fighters, bombers and reconnaissance types. Richthofen's combat report (illustrated) provided details about his own aeroplane, information about his 66th victim, and confirmed victories of other pilots: 'I took off with 30 aeroplanes of my

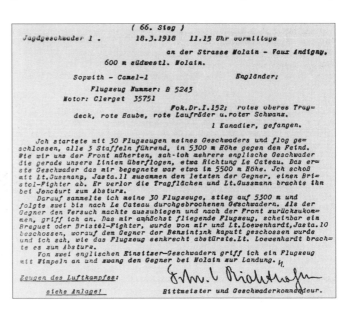

Geschwader as a unit, leading all three Staffeln at 5,300 metres' altitude against the enemy. As we approached the Front, I saw several British groups that had just crossed our lines, [heading] in the general direction of Le Cateau. The first group that I encountered was at about 5,500 metres' altitude. Together with Leutnant Gussmann of Jasta 11, I shot down the last opponent [in the formation], a Bristol Fighter. It lost its wings and Leutnant Gussmann brought it crashing down at Joncourt.[45]

'After that, I regrouped my 30 aeroplanes, climbed to 5,300 metres and followed towards Le Cateau the two [enemy] groups that had broken through. When the opponent made an attempt to turn away and come back to the Front, I attacked. The next aeroplane flying closest to me, apparently a Bréguet or a Bristol Fighter, was fired at by me and Leutnant Löwenhardt of Jasta 10, whereupon the opponent's fuel tank was shot to pieces and I saw the aeroplane go straight down. Leutnant Löwenhardt caused it to crash.[46]

'Out of two British single-seat groups I attacked an aeroplane with pennants [fluttering from the struts] and forced the opponent to land near Molain.'[47]

Below: March was an eventful month for Jasta 6 leader Wilhelm Reinhard. Unbeknown to him, on the 10th, Richthofen wrote an order designating Reinhard to succeed him in the event of his not returning from a flight.[48] On the 12th, this native of Düsseldorf marked his 27th birthday, a few days after that he survived the rough landing and somersault that wiped out his Fokker Dr.I, as seen here, and on the 22nd he was promoted to Hauptmann.[49] Four weeks and three days later Richthofen's succession order had to be implemented and Reinhard became JG I's second Kommandeur [see Appendix I]. On that occasion, in a letter home he pledged: 'My goal will now be to influence the Geschwader by personal example, i.e., to shoot down more [enemy aeroplanes] than anyone else. When [I was] with Jasta 6, I could shoot down [opponents] calmly and take my time. I intended to relax after my 16th victory. That [thought] has been dropped. For two to three months long my hands and my feet have been bandaged [because of severe wounds received in combat on 4 September 1917] and when I get up every morning I wish for good weather so that we can [engage in] air fights ...'[50]

7 — The Last Patrol

Right: Although indulging in an occasional cigarette, Manfred von Richthofen (fourth from right) led an otherwise healthy lifestyle. According to his brother Lothar: 'Immediately after eating and when flight operations allowed, he took a half-hour nap in the afternoon; for, in the period of peak activity that we had then, frequently we flew five to seven times a day. In order to keep up that pace, it was fundamental to eat, sleep and not have a drop of alcohol.'[1] The distance from photographer to subject here indicates that Richthofen may have been taken by surprise during a visit to Jagdstaffel 10 members at their new facilities at Awoingt. On 20 March 1918, the day before the last major German offensive of the war began, Jagdgeschwader I moved to the advance airfield, just off the main road from Cambrai to Le Cateau. Joining in this relaxed moment were, from left: Vizefeldwebel Paul Aue; Leutnant der Reserve Julius Bender; Leutnant der Reserve Julius Grassmann; Oberleutnant Erich Löwenhardt; Oberleutnant Karl Bodenschatz; Leutnant der Reserve Max Kühn; Richthofen; Oberleutnant Hugo Schäfer; Leutnant der Reserve Fritz Friedrichs; Gefreiter Alfons Nitsche.

Right: The German offensive – code-named Operation 'Michael' – began at 0445 hours on 21 March. Heavy fog provided perfect cover for advancing German infantry, but hampered Jagdgeschwader I's flight operations and few victories were recorded. It was not until three days later that Richthofen had success in aerial combat. In an afternoon encounter on the 24th, he was flying this aircraft – Fokker Dr.I 477/17– at the head of a 25-strong formation that pounced on ten S.E.5a fighters. Given the overwhelming strength of the Germans, when Richthofen closed in on one British fighter, it had no chance and, as he recorded,

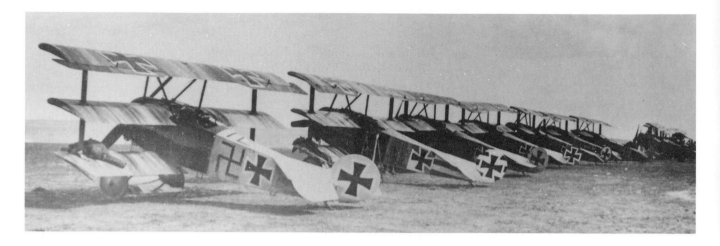

was dispatched in short order: 'During a long single-seater fight ... I attacked an Englishman at an altitude of 2,500 metres. Both wings broke away in [the stream of] my machine-gun fire. The remnants were dispersed in the vicinity of Combles.'[2] Richthofen was credited with his 67th victory.

Above: JG I did not remain long at Awoingt. On 26 March, eager to stay close to the advancing ground forces, Richthofen had Geschwader facilities relocated westward to Léchelle, where this photograph of a Jasta 11 Fokker Triplane line-up was taken. The variety of colours and individual markings makes clear why Allied airmen referred to the Geschwader as the Flying Circus. Adjutant Karl Bodenschatz recorded: 'Formerly this had been a British airfield, but five days earlier the "Lords" had squeezed the aeroplanes beneath their elegant breeches and had to abscond. With sublime anticipation the Geschwader roars in here; they are said to have indulged in fantastic luxuries, these Lords. But the young German gentlemen overflow with biting comments when they look at matters more closely. It is a rather neglected place, with wretched barracks, [and] primitive, plain corrugated-metal

huts; the British seem to have disdained window glass and wood; in its place, ample amounts of oil paper are pasted on to every opening. To make up for that, at least [our men] find some choice blankets and some very fine cloth of a quality not seen for a long time. Moreover, all the [aircraft] are accommodated very well and comfortably in four large tent hangars, and that has some value.'[3]

Below: Typical of politicians of any era, the initial success of the spring offensive inspired members of the *Reichstag* [Parliament] to visit the battle zone to be seen with Richthofen (centre). According to Jasta 4 leader Ernst Udet, a gala dinner featured long speeches, after which much wine – not touched by the pilots under Richthofen's watchful eye – assured the

him that engendered trust and a lifetime of fond memories. Leutnant Gisbert-Wilhelm Groos, a former Uhlan like his Kommandeur, was a 7-victory veteran of Jagdstaffeln 4 and 11, as well as a Richthofen protégé and Staffel leader. Some 40 years after the end of the war, Groos summed up what many former JG I members felt about the man they remembered with pride and affection as *der Rittmeister*: 'Richthofen was a born leader. Sharp as a razor in service matters; at all times fair, especially in the air over the Front. He saw everything. He gave new men in the Jasta every chance to score a victory. He gave away many victories, if by doing so the young pilot was able to score his first "kill". He protected every member of the flight, if possible, but there was no pardon if a pilot sneaked away from a fight. That pilot would be transferred immediately. On the ground, after duty [hours], Richthofen was like a boy with a wonderful sense of humour.'[5]

legislators a deep sleep that night. JG I mischief-makers had other ideas. After the guests had settled in their beds, several pilots approached their quarters, firing blank ammunition and flares. Udet recalled the impression of 'a clattering of gun fire and the dull thud of bombs being detonated. Right after that, an outcry ... We stood hidden in the dark shadows of the other barracks. Suddenly, across the way, the door flew open and out charged three forms in flapping white nightshirts. The Rittmeister laughed so hard that tears ran down his cheeks. "Air raid! Back into the barracks!" thundered a mighty voice across the airfield and, in a frantic run, the three white forms disappeared back behind the door. The next morning they got under way hurriedly. They did not even have breakfast with us. We laughed for a long time afterwards. Joys [at the Front] are very few and whenever there is a chance for some fun, one enjoys it gratefully and for a long time ...'[4]

Below: While JG I members settled into Bell tents left behind by Léchelle's former Royal Flying Corps residents, Manfred von Richthofen's and the Geschwader's victory tallies continued to climb. The Kommandeur was the most visible element of

Above: Some air commanders earned respect through fear; others, such as Richthofen, were respected for their admirable qualities. Whether playing a practical joke on visiting politicians or playing with his dog Moritz, as seen here at Léchelle airfield, Richthofen had a warmth about

the unit and, following the three-day period during which he scored his 68th to 73rd victories, he was singled out for praise by the Commanding General of the Air Force: 'I have expressed my and the Air Force's congratulations to the father of Rittmeister Freiherr von Richthofen on [the occasion of] the 100th aerial victory of both brothers. To Leutnants Udet and Löwenhardt, who in quick succession and [with] exemplary zest for action, have continued to increase the number of their victories, I also express my sincere appreciation. The 27th of March was once again a proud day for Jagdgeschwader I.'[6]

Below: Great Britain's Royal Air Force was formed on 1 April 1918 by the amalgamation of the Royal Flying Corps and Royal Naval Air Service. Jasta 11 marked the occasion by recording its 250th triumph, a Sopwith F.1 Camel brought down south of Sailly-Laurette by Leutnant Hans Joachim Wolff. Next day, Manfred von Richthofen marked a milestone of his own: victory No. 75.[7] His hometown newspaper, *Breslauer Zeitung*, reported the event as the leading story of its 3 April edition, seen here. For all the fame and glory aerial combat brought, however, by this

time warfare was beginning to have emotional and physical effects on the JG I Kommandeur. Oberleutnant Peter Martin Lampel, a visiting bomber pilot, later recalled his candid conversation with Richthofen: 'That morning the Rittmeister had shot down his 75th. He told me that it had been a bitter battle; he had got right up to five metres away from the enemy, who then went down burning. "It is a strange feeling," he said. "There, once again, a pair of men shot dead; they lie somewhere out there all burned up and I myself sit here every day at the table and the food tastes as good as ever. I once said that to His Majesty when I was ordered to dine with the Kaiser … [who] said nothing to me except: "My soldiers do not shoot men dead; my soldiers annihilate the opponents!"'[8]

Opposite page, top: Four days later, Richthofen led a Jasta 11 Flight over the Somme sector in this aeroplane – Fokker Dr.I 127/18 – and caught a Flight of British fighters strafing and bombing German troops north-east of Villers-Brettoneux. Richthofen zeroed in on one of the single-seaters and scored his 76th victory.[9] His string of successes seemed to be endless, although people closest to him knew that he needed a rest. Jasta 6 leader Hauptmann Wilhelm Reinhard noted that, when it came to combat flying, the Kommandeur's father 'never told his sons to stop or preached caution to them. Only once – and this was after the 75th aerial victory of his eldest son – did he suggest that now it was enough and that [Manfred] should slow down in shooting down aeroplanes. One could take this to be an omen. But our Rittmeister was of the opinion that as Geschwader-Kommandeur he was obligated to his men by example and [his own sense of] daring to be in the thick of it with them.'[10]

Below: The fight on 6 April impressed Leutnant der Reserve Richard Wenzl, whose aeroplane is second from right in this line-up. The pilots are, from left: Unteroffizier Robert Eiserbeck (KiA 12 April), Leutnant der Reserve Hans Weiss and Vizefeldwebel Edgar Scholz (both KiA 2 May). Wenzl wrote: 'As Léchelle lay too far back for Richthofen and he always wanted to be at the source [of activity], an advance airfield was selected at Harbonnières ... about six kilometres behind the lines. Every morning we flew there, stayed over that area the whole day and in the evening flew back home again ... On the 6th of April there was proper flying weather again ... [and] I will never forget this first flight under Richthofen's leadership ... I was delighted by the way Richthofen led. He worked the controls of his superlative engine in such a way that one could keep up with him and not zoom ahead of him. It was clear to me that, after a long time away [from flying], I was just becoming accustomed to my [aerial] "vision"

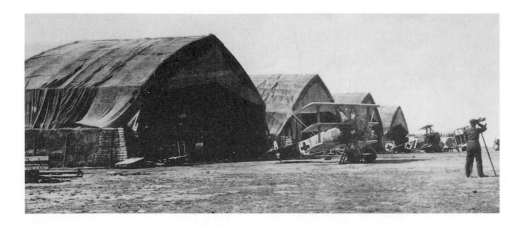

again. So I was not astonished when Richthofen suddenly made some conspicuous movements with his red machine – a sign that the air was not completely clear. We were already on to some [enemy aircraft] and Richthofen set his on fire ...'[11]

Above: Jasta 6 Fokker Triplanes, seen here in front of Bessonneau hangers left behind by the RFC at Léchelle, accompanied Jasta 11 on Sunday, 7 April. That day, a pilot from each Staffel was credited with a victory, while the Geschwader-Kommandeur added two to his score. Because of the imperfect nature of recording air combat successes, questions remain about Richthofen's claims, which at the time were accepted without comment. Second Lieutenant Robert R. Rowe, one of eighteen Sopwith F.1 Camel pilots in action with No. 73 Squadron that day, reported that at 1150 hours: 'Whilst on Offensive Patrol over enemy lines east of Villers-Brettoneux ... [we] encountered an enemy formation of about 20 Fokker Triplanes, one of which I dived on and fired about 150 rounds into it. I saw my tracers enter E.A. at about [the] pilot's seat, and watched E.A. fall about 2,000 ft. out of control.[12] I then left this machine in order to assist one of our formation, who was being attacked by

one Fokker Triplane. I fired a short burst at this machine, which then dived away into a cloud.'[13] Richthofen claimed a SPAD at 1205 hours north of Villers-Brettoneux; there were no SPADs in the area, but a Sopwith Camel, possibly the one reported under attack by Lieutenant Rowe, went down *west* of Villers- Brettoneux. The pilot was uninjured and returned to his own lines, unaware that he may have been counted as Richthofen's 78th victim.[14]

Below: Richthofen was credited with shooting down eight Sopwith F.1 Camels, but most likely not the aircraft flown by Lieutenant Ronald Adam – even though the British actor and author was informed that *he* was the Red Baron's 78th victim. Adam flew to France in the aeroplane seen here – B.9307 of No. 44 Squadron – on 30 March. Eight days later while flying a new machine with No. 73 Squadron, he was shot down by a JG I Fokker Triplane. Adam smashed into a railway line at the intersection of the old Roman Road and the main road from Proyart to Harbonnières – 12 kilometres north-east of the spot where Richthofen said his 78th victim fell. That evening a German orderly

visited the British pilot in confinement and greeted him with the news: 'Freiherr von Richthofen's compliments. You are his 79th [sic] victory.'[15] The Kommandeur liked to contact his surviving victims and Adam may have received this dubious honour in the absence of firm confirmation of Richthofen's 77th and 78th victories. 'It was little consolation to learn that I had fought with von Richthofen or that he was killed two weeks later, to the day,' Adam wrote to the author. 'I was more concerned with the business of staying alive, as I was transported further behind the German lines.'[16]

Right: JG I moved to a new airfield at Cappy on 12 April. The change and administrative duties kept Richthofen from scoring again until 20 April, when he shot down two Sopwith F.1 Camels within minutes of each other. He led six triplanes of Jasta 11 against a larger force of RAF fighters and, once the air battle had begun, he saw one of his men under attack by a skilled British pilot. The Kommandeur went to his comrade's assistance and slipped in behind a British fighter piloted by Major Richard Raymond-Barker, MC, a five-victory ace. "I put myself behind the opponent and brought him down on fire with only a few shots. The enemy aeroplane crashed near Hamel Wood, where it burned further,' Richthofen wrote.[17] Then, as recorded in his last combat report, illustrated here: 'Three minutes after I shot down the first [enemy aeroplane] in flames, I attacked a second Camel from the same squadron. The opponent let his machine fall, recovered and repeated this manoeuvre several times. [Following him] all the while, I approached as closely as combat would allow and fired about 50 rounds [until it] caught fire. The fuselage burned in the air, [and] the remnants crashed north-east of Villers-Brettoneux.'

Right: On Sunday, 21 April 1918, Rittmeister von Richthofen prepared for what would be his last flight. The day after his 80th victory, mischievous JG I

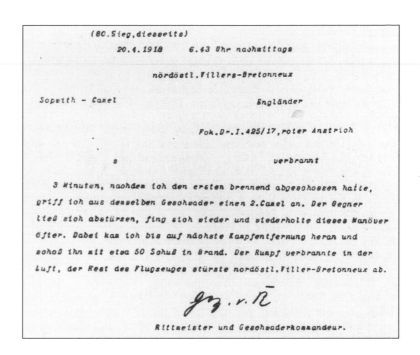

members 'got together and tied a wheelchock to the tail of Moritz, [his] big dog, so that the poor creature, now so encumbered, would seek solace from his comforter,' Geschwader-Adjutant Karl Bodenschatz

noted about events reminiscent of this view.[18] For Richthofen himself, however, light moments were scarce, as he wrote shortly before his death about his book *Der rote Kampfflieger*: 'I now have the deepest impression ... that people have been exposed to quite another Richthofen than I truly am deep inside myself. When I read [my] book, I smile at my own insolence. I am no longer so insolent in spirit. Not because I can imagine how it would be one day when death is breathing down my neck ... although I have thought ... often enough that it can happen. I have been told by [people in] high places that I should give up flying, for one day it will catch up with me. I would be miserable with myself if now, burdened with glory and decorations, I were to become a pensioner of my own dignity in order to save my precious life for the nation, while every poor fellow in the trenches endures his duty as I do mine.'[19]

Below: On its arrival at JG I, Richthofen's all-red Fokker Dr.I 425/17 had sported a fresh coat of paint, but this was well worn by the time of his final flight in it. Ground fog in the area precluded an early morning patrol over the lines on 21 April, but it was clearing at 1030 hours when two Geschwader Flights took off to intercept British aeroplanes reported heading for their sector. The Kommandeur led a

Flight which included Leutnant Hans Joachim Wolff, who recorded that, at the Front, they 'saw seven Sopwith Camels ... [and] above us were seven more ... some of which attacked Jasta 5, some of which remained above. One or two came at us. We began to fight. In the course of the fight I saw that Herr Rittmeister was often near me, but he had not yet shot at anything ... While Oberleutnant [Walther] Karjus and I fought against two or three Camels, suddenly I saw the red machine near me, as he fired at a Camel that first went into a spin, [and] then slipped away in a steep dive toward the west ... We had a rather strong east wind and ... as the Camel went down, I looked over at Herr Rittmeister and saw that he was at extremely low altitude over the Somme near Corbie, right behind an Englishman.'[20]

Right: Richthofen's intended 81st victim was 23-year-old Second Lieutenant Wilfrid R. May of No. 209 Squadron. The Canadian pilot, seen here during training in 1917, was on his first combat mission and had been told to observe the action from a distance. Imprudently, he dived on a German fighter and, when his guns jammed, he headed for home. Machine-gun fire from behind him alerted May that he was being pursued. Looking round, he saw an all-red Fokker Triplane behind him. May recalled: 'I kept on dodging and spinning. I imagine from about 12,000 feet until I ran out of sky and had to hedge-hop over the ground. Richthofen was firing at me continually ... [and when] we came over the German lines, troops fired at us as we went over, [and] this was also the case coming over the British lines. I got [down along] the Somme River and started [flying] up the valley at a very low altitude. Richthofen was very

close on my tail. I went around a curve in the river, just near Corbie, [but] Richthofen beat me to it and came over the hill. At that point I was a sitting duck ... I felt that he had me cold ... I looked around again and saw Richthofen do a spin and half and hit the ground. I looked up and saw one of our machines directly behind. I joined up with him and returned to our [aerodrome].'[21]

Above: right Captain A. Roy Brown, leader of 'A' Flight of No. 209 Squadron, had nine confirmed victories to his credit when he took off on 21 April 1918. Some historians contend that, in helping fellow-Canadian 'Wop' May, Brown scored a tenth victory and it was the Fokker Triplane flown by Manfred von Richthofen. May's combat report indi-

cated that he thought so: 'I ... was attacked by a Red triplane which chased me over the lines low to the ground. While he was on my tail, Captain Brown attacked and shot it down. I observed it crash into the ground.'[22] No other report supports May's later recollection that he saw Richthofen's aeroplane 'do a spin and a half' prior to coming down near Australian troops. Another aerial witness, Lieutenant [later Air Vice-Marshal Sir] Francis Mellersh, reported that 'a bright red triplane crashed quite close to me and in looking up I saw Captain Brown.'[23] Brown's own report alluded to a victory claim by stating that he 'dived on [a] pure red triplane which was firing on Lieut. May. I got a long burst into him and he went down vertical and was observed to crash by Lieut. Mellersh and Lieut. May.'[24]

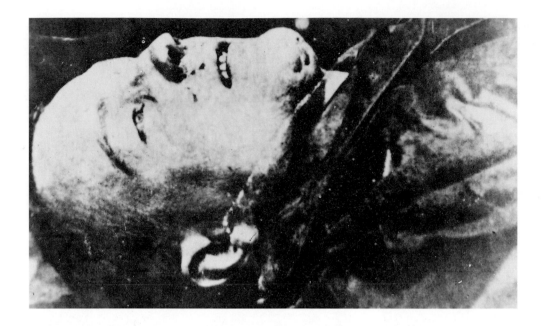

demise. According to a British prisoner's statement in the weekly German air intelligence summary, credit for shooting him down 'has been contested for some time, but the official inquiry has determined that Richthofen had pursued an R.E.8 until it was close to the ground, whereupon a Camel attacked him from behind and shot him down ... The prisoner hoped that it was not believed on the German side that a British pilot accepted prize money that a British newspaper offered to whoever shot down Richthofen.'[25]

Above: Manfred von Richthofen was killed at about 1145 hours German Time (one hour ahead of Allied Time). He came down in a beet field at Vaux-sur-Somme, along the road from Corbie to Bray, and was dead when Australian troops reached the crash site. His body was removed from his aeroplane and taken some fifteen kilometres away, to Poulainville airfield, where it was examined and where this photograph was taken. Based at that airfield was No. 3 Squadron, Australian Flying Corps, an R.E.8 unit which had engaged JG I Fokker Triplanes that morning and was perceived as having been involved in Richthofen's

Below: In death, Richthofen the inveterate souvenir hunter became the object of many like-minded people in the area. Even though his aeroplane was reported to have landed nearly intact, it was soon stripped to pieces, as evident in this view. Many Germans accepted Australian claims of shooting down the red triplane, including Air Force Commanding General Ernst von Hoeppner, who wrote: 'Following the pursuit of an opponent at low altitude, while flying behind the enemy Front, apparently [Richthofen] was caught in the machine-gun fire of an Australian battery.'[26] Support for the ground gunners' claim came from Captain N. C. Graham and Lieutenant G. E. Downs, Army doctors attached to the RAF, who examined Richthofen's body and reported: 'The entrance wound was ... on the right side of the chest in the anterior fold of the armpit; the exit wound was ... at a slightly higher level near the front of the chest, the point of exit being about half an inch below the left nipple and about three-quarters of an inch external to it. From the nature of the exit wound, we think that the bullet passed straight through the chest from right to left ... The gun firing this bullet must have been situated in roughly the same plane as the long axis of the German machine, and fired from the right and slightly behind the right of Captain [*sic*] Richthofen.'[27]

Below: Following a brief examination of the wounds, Richthofen's body was laid out on a piece of corrugated metal, as depicted here. During the evening of 21 April, various Australian, British and Canadian airmen came through the hangar to pay their respects to their former foe. Other soldiers came in from time to time to search through the dead flyer's effects and steal whatever items

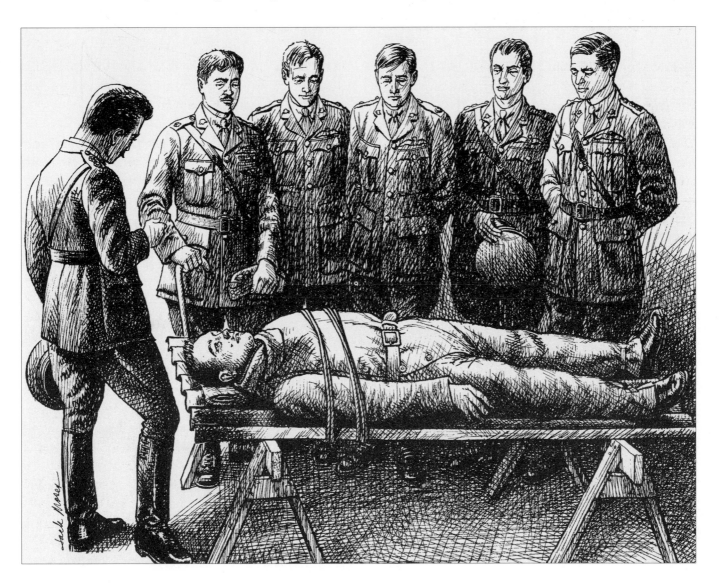

compliant guards would allow. Captain A. Roy Brown, who was certain he had killed Richthofen and yet claimed he had not seen the body, wrote home a few days later: 'It was rather [odd] about Richthofen being shot down. The infantry on the ground, the anti-aircraft and an Australian Squadron put in reports that they had shot him down. All reports differed. They had a medical examination of the body and it was found they were all wrong without the slightest doubt. It is a terrible thing when you think of it that they should examine a body to see who should have the credit [for] killing him. What I saw that day shook me up quite a lot, as it was the first time I have seen a man whom I know I had killed. If you don't shoot them, they will shoot you [and] so it has to be done.'[28]

Below: On the afternoon of 22 April, ten days before Manfred von Richthofen's 26th birthday, he was buried with full military honours in the local cemetery at Bertangles, alongside the airfield used by No. 209 Squadron. Six Australian pilots – all Captains – carried the plain, black-painted coffin bearing Richthofen's remains. Among the RAF officers attending was Major W. Sholto Douglas [later Marshal of the Royal Air Force Lord Douglas of

Kirtleside], at that time Commanding Officer of No. 84 Squadron, who recalled: 'It was with mixed feelings that I watched the burial of the great German ace, for it was impossible not to feel a little emotional about it … Richthofen was undoubtedly a gallant pilot, although he always fought with the utmost caution – except for his very last scrap – and he never hesitated to avoid a fight or pull out of one if he thought the odds against him were too great. He always had his highly trained Circus behind him, protecting him from attack from the rear, and that enabled him to devote the whole of his attention to shooting down his victims. It is possible that this lack of caution about keeping an eye on what was happening behind him was the reason why he did not see Roy Brown coming down on him.'[29]

Top right: No. 3 Squadron, AFC, contributed a broken R.E.8 propeller to be fashioned into a Christian symbol suitable for Richthofen's grave marker. The choice of aeroplane was fitting, because the German ace had emerged victorious from seven fights with R.E.8s and he had great respect for their defensive capabilities. Major W. Sholto Douglas, whose squadron was based at Bertangles, had high regard for Richthofen's abilities and expressed an entirely practical view of what the German ace's death meant to RAF units at the Front: 'We were all glad enough, in our hearts, that Richthofen was out of the way. He had been a thorn in our sides, it seemed, for such a long time. After his death his place as leader of the Circus was taken by [Hauptmann] Wilhelm Reinhard, an army officer from before the outbreak of war who had seen a great deal of service and who had been severely wounded at least twice. Two months later Reinhard was

killed in a flying accident while testing a new type of fighter, and the Circus was then placed under the command of Hermann Göring. That led to our continuing to engage each other, as we had for some time past, in yet further brisk exchanges in the air.'[30] A few days after the funeral, the gravemarker was stolen and has not since re-appeared.

Lower left: Most Richthofen souvenirs passed away into a vast network of First World War survivors, their families and friends. Over the years many of those items have been collected by private individuals and, when they have surfaced at auctions in recent times, the various Red Baron mementoes have fetched high prices. Some objects too cumbersome to be removed easily in 1918 – such as the Oberursel UR II rotary engine of his Fokker Dr.I – remain in official or governmental custody for viewing by the general public and study by historians. The engine, for example, is in the collection of the Imperial War Museum in London. It is the largest single piece of the aircraft to survive intact.

Below: To cope with low temperatures at high altitudes, many First World War flyers wore fur-lined flight-suits and boots. Manfred von Richthofen had a pair of distinctive-looking fur boots (see page 102),

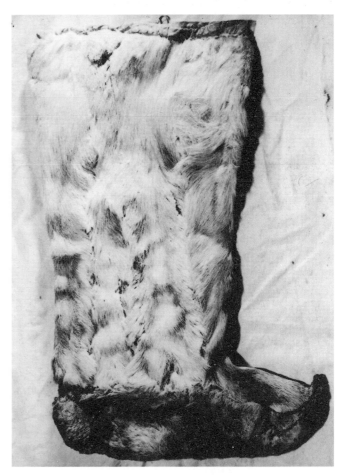

one of which survives in the Australian War Memorial in Canberra.

Right: The seat of Fokker Dr.I 425/17 was awarded as a trophy to Captain A. Roy Brown, the putative victor over Richthofen. In turn, he presented it to the Royal Canadian Military Institute at Toronto. Large portions of the Triplane's fabric bearing the German national insignia also survived, most of it going to museums in Australia and Canada. One large piece is in private hands, having been acquired at auction in recent years.

Right: It took three days for news of Richthofen's death to appear in the German press. The *Schlesische Zeitung* in Breslau gave the news a Page 1 banner headline in its edition of 24 April. Articles also appeared in national and overseas newspapers, but no doubt the coverage was given greater prominence in the city of Richthofen's birth. Under the subheadline '*Der Heldentod Richthofens*' [Richthofen's Heroic Death] at left is a wire service story explaining the delay in reporting the news: 'On 21 April, Rittmeister Manfred Freiherr von Richthofen did not return from a fighter patrol over the Somme. According to collaborating accounts by his companions and observers on the ground, Richthofen was diving in pursuit with his fighter aeroplane to very low altitude when it appeared that engine trouble forced him to land behind enemy lines. As the landing took place smoothly, the hope persisted

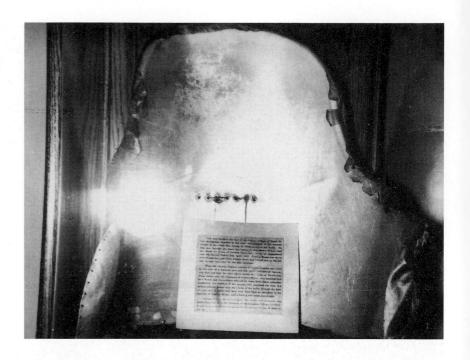

that Richthofen was taken prisoner uninjured. A report by Reuters [news agency] on the 23rd of April, however, left no doubt that Rittmeister Freiherr von Richthofen had met his death. Since Richthofen would not have been hit easily from the air while in pursuit, it seems that he was the victim of a lucky shot from the ground. According to the British report, Richthofen was buried with military honours on the 22nd of April in a churchyard in the vicinity of where he came down.'

Above: On the 26th anniversary of Manfred von Richthofen's birth – 2 May 1918 – the fallen hero was honoured in an official memorial service held in the *Garnisonkirche* [Garrison Church] in Berlin. The old church was steeped in German military legend and a fitting place for the Fatherland to pay tribute to a brave son. In the absence of a coffin, a catafalque bore the black felt *Ordenskissen* [Orders Cushion] with the medals and awards Richthofen had received from Prussia, other German kingdoms and states, and Central Powers allies. Richthofen's repose in French soil was disturbed after the war, when his remains were transferred to a military cemetery set aside for fallen Germans in Fricourt, east of Albert. The Richthofen family hoped to bring Manfred's remains home to Schweidnitz to join those of his father, who died in 1920, and his brother Lothar, who was killed while piloting an airliner in 1922. National sentiment held otherwise and on 14 November 1925 Manfred's remains were exhumed from Fricourt and, two days later, transported along a circuitous route through Germany and to Berlin, where the honour guard of eight *Pour le Mérite* flyers, seen here, waited to escort the coffin through the capital and to the *Gnadenkirche* [Church of Mercy].

Left: Bolko Freiherr von Richthofen, who represented the family in making the funeral arrangements, later wrote: 'On Thursday morning [19 November] the body lay in state in the *Gnadenkirche*. The zinc coffin [bearing Manfred's remains] had been placed in a brown oak casket, Uhlan swords and *Tschapkas* [Uhlan dress helmets] lay on the coffin. In front of the coffin stood the wooden cross that had marked Manfred's grave in Fricourt. It bore only his name and the number 53091. The honour guard included men who had been officers in his Jagdgeschwader and in Ulanen-Regiment Nr 1. Berliners filed past the coffin in unbroken succession the whole day.'[31] Pilots seen here were (left) Leutnant der Reserve Josef Veltjens, former Kommandeur of JG II, and Leutnant der Reserve Kurt Wüsthoff, whom Richthofen had had to remove from command of Jasta 4.

Right: The most significant item from the funeral returned to the family was Manfred's *Ordenskissen*, seen here on display in the Richthofen Museum in Schweidnitz. The ageing Generalfeldmarschall Paul von Beneckendorf und von Hindenburg, by then President of Germany, wore his own many medals and uniform to lead the nation in mourning during the interment on 20 November. Bolko von Richthofen recalled: 'The ceremony at the church was short and dignified. Then eight flyers, all knights of the *Orden Pour le Mérite*, raised the coffin to a gun carriage of Prussian Artillerie-Regiment Nr 2. A company of the sentries was set at the head and with muffled drums the procession went along streets lined with [members of] countless organisations to the *Invalidenfriedhof* [Cemetery for the Disabled]. An earlier regimental comrade who was now a member of the Reichswehr walked in front of the coffin and carried the cushion bearing the decorations that had been awarded to Manfred during his lifetime. Above the cemetery aeroplanes crossed paths trailing black pennants and the honour guard fired the last salute three times. While the Reichswehr Chorus sang the "Song of Good Comrades", the coffin sank into the earth.'[32]

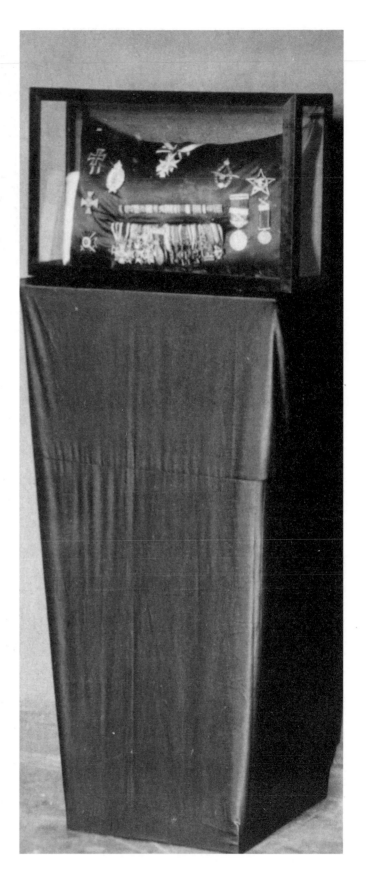

Right: The Richthofen family lived at No. 10 Striegauer Strasse in Schweidnitz. After the First World War, the street was renamed Manfred-von-Richthofen-Strasse and, on the 15th anniversary of his death, the family home became a private museum open to the public. Freifrau von Richthofen, aided by family members, showed visitors through rooms filled with trophies and mementoes attesting to the success of Manfred and Lothar von Richthofen (see pages 27, 53 and 60). British journalist John C. Hook wrote at the time: 'The Museum ... takes up the whole of the first floor, which includes the room where Manfred slept and which he fitted up himself with the many souvenirs he brought home when on leave ... At the entrance an attendant sold me a ticket and numerous postcards, as well as a leaflet, written by Freifrau von Richthofen, describing the exact manner in which her son was killed. On ascending the stairs, which are decorated with hunting trophies of the Richthofen family, I arrived in a long corridor from which five rooms all led off ... .'[33] At the end of his visit, Hook observed: 'I left Freifrau von Richthofen sitting sad-faced and alone in her garden, dreaming perhaps of those days when Manfred and Lothar laughed and played in this house of memories.'[34]

Schweidnitz Striegauerstraße
Elternhaus unseres größten Kampffliegers
Rittmeister Manfred Freiherr von Richthofen.

Right: In addition to the museum, Manfred von Richthofen and his considerable achievements were once honoured by this memorial in Schweidnitz. Following the Red Army's drive through Silesia in 1945, the bronze plaque disappeared, the cemetery containing the graves of Albrecht and Lothar von Richthofen was ploughed over, and the entire contents of the Richthofen Museum were seized and shipped to the former Soviet Union with other war booty. Most German Silesians were forced to flee or were expelled as the victorious Soviets re-drew the map of Europe and ceded this and other territory to Poland in exchange for Polish land annexed by the USSR. With the collapse of communism, the democratisation of much of Eastern Europe and growing German friendship and co-operation with former Soviet states, it is more likely that some – or perhaps even all – of the Richthofen aviation history treasures will be restored to their rightful owners and be displayed in response to growing interest in the Red Baron and his life and times.

Appendix I — People Associated with Richthofen

Right: Oberleutnant Georg Zeumer, an original member of *Brieftauben-Abteilung* Ostende, seen here near the unit's special train, was Manfred von Richthofen's first pilot in combat. After a short time with Richthofen as his observer in Feldflieger-Abteilung 69 in Russia, Zeumer returned to the BAO in Flanders. On 21 August 1915, Richthofen was assigned to the same unit and wrote: 'My good friend Zeumer picked me up at the railway station in Brussels ... We flew a lot, but seldom had aerial combats and never any successes.'

An example is the flight on 1 September, he recalled: 'Suddenly, I spotted a Farman, nonchalantly flying its reconnaissance mission. My heart beat furiously as Zeumer approached it. I was excited at what was about to take place. I had never seen an aerial combat and I had only a vague conception of it ... Before I knew what was happening, both the Englishman and we rushed by each other. I had fired at best four shots when the Englishman suddenly got behind us and shot the works at us. I ..... did not have the feeling of danger because I could not truly imagine the final result of such a battle. We went around each other several times until, finally, to our great astonishment, the Englishman cheerfully turned away from us and flew off. I was greatly disappointed, as was my pilot.'[1]

Right: Rittmeister Erich Graf von Holck, Richthofen's second pilot, taught his observer important elements of character. Many German officers

kept dogs, but here Holck poses with his *'Lieblingskatze'* [favourite cat] at the Front and, just for show, a lion cub. 'Graf von Holck was not merely a sportsman on the ground,' Richthofen wrote. 'By all appearances, flying gave him more than a little pleasure. He was a pilot of rare ability ... [who] grossly outclassed his enemies. We flew many fine reconnaissances – who knows how far? – into Russia. I never felt more secure with so young a pilot; moreover, he was a great support in critical moments. When I turned round and looked into his determined face, I had even more courage than before. My last flight with him nearly went awry ... A gigantic pillar of smoke that rose up to some 2,000 metres prevented us from completing our mission as, in order to see better, we were at only 1,500 metres' altitude. Holck thought about this for a moment. I asked him what he wanted to do and advised him to fly around it, which would have been perhaps a detour of five minutes. But Holck would have none of it. On the contrary: the greater the danger, the more it appealed to him. Therefore, he flew right through it! It was fun for me to be together with such a daring fellow.'[2] Seven months later, Richthofen watched helplessly from a distance as a swarm of French fighters attacked Holck's Fokker Eindecker and killed him.

Right: Anthony H. G. Fokker flew an aeroplane of his own design when, at the age of 20, he qualified for Deutsche Luftfahrer Verband [German Air Travellers' Association] pilot's licence No. 88 on 7 June 1911. He was born in Kediri, Java, the son of a Dutch coffee plantation owner and when his father retired and returned to the Netherlands, Fokker pursued his education and then his career in Germany.[3] Age did not deter him from setting up his own company and becoming a supplier of German fighter aeroplanes. His own abilities enabled him to become friends with pilots, as noted by Max Immelmann, then an unproven combat flyer with Feldflieger-Abteilung 62, in his letter of 25 June 1915: 'In recent times we have received two small combat monoplanes from the Fokker factory. Primarily to see these fighting machines, Crown Prince [Rupprecht] of Bavaria was at our airfield yesterday and inspected us and [Feld-flieger-] Abteilung 20. Director Fokker, the builder of the combat aircraft, was presented to him. [Fokker], as well as Leutnant [Otto] Parschau, flew the aeroplane and fired from the air at the ground. Fokker especially amazed us with his skill.'[4]

Right: Oberleutnant Max Immelmann was an early fighter ace who influenced Manfred von Richthofen and other German pilots of the First World War. When the war began, Immelmann was a reserve officer candidate in a rail transport unit, but his pre-war studies in mechanical engineering qualified the 23-year-old Saxon for the pilot training offered in the Inspectorate of Aviation announcement of 10 August 1914. Immelmann flew two-seat reconnaissance aeroplanes beginning in March 1915 and his aggres-

enemy aeroplanes and gained a chest-full of decorations, including Prussia's *Orden Pour le Mérite*, which is said to have gained the nickname 'the blue Max' because its bright enamel finish reflected that colour against the pilot's pale skin. He was 25 years old when he was killed in aerial combat on 18 June 1916.

Below: Hauptmann Oswald Boelcke, who also began as a ground officer and switched to aviation, was Immelmann's partner and competitor. Boelcke completed flight training just as Germany was mobilising for war and soon showed his bravery in combat. He was an early recipient of the Iron Cross 2nd Class and 1st Class awards when both were still significant decorations. He was senior to Immelmann when they were in Feldflieger-Abteilung 62 and was the first of the pair to shoot down an enemy aeroplane. Boelcke and Immelmann were the first German pilots to receive the *Pour le Mérite*, on the same day,

sive nature earned him a posting to Feldflieger-Abteilung 62, equipped with new single-seat fighters. His brother Franz, also a pilot, described the allure of these early machines: 'This small single-seat fighter from the Fokker Works in Schwerin was the great surprise for our opponents. An 80-horsepower rotary engine, which weighed only some 300 kilograms, gave the Eindecker a speed of about 130 kilometres per hour and ability to climb to about 3,500 metres (its ceiling) in an hour. These flying qualities, amazing for 1915, were paired with great manoeuvrability and outstandingly constructed armament.'[5] During his ten-month air combat career in Fokker Eindeckers, Max Immelmann shot down fifteen

12 January 1916. After Immelmann's death, Boelcke was sent on an official visit to Turkey and then recalled to the Western Front to develop and lead the fighter unit Jagdstaffel 2. En route back to France, he visited his brother Wilhelm, a section leader at the bomber wing Kampfgeschwader 2 on the Russian Front, where Oswald selected two promising pilots for his new command: Erwin Böhme and Manfred von Richthofen. Less than three months later, 40-victory ace Boelcke collided with Böhme while pursuing a British fighter and fell to his death. Boelcke was 25, as was Immelmann, when he died and the age that Manfred von Richthofen would attain before he too perished.

Below: Leutnant der Reserve Erwin Böhme escaped injury in the mid-air accident that ended Boelcke's life. His letter describing the crash mentioned Richthofen's incidental role in events on 28 October

1916: 'In the fierce aerial combat ... during which we had only a brief time to fire, we sought to drive down [the enemy aeroplanes] by alternately cutting them off, as we had already done so often with success. Boelcke and I had an Englishman right between us, when another opponent pursued by friend Richthofen cut in front of us. During the simultaneous lightning-quick evasive manoeuvre, Boelcke and I, obstructed by our wings, could not see each other for an instant ... How can I describe for you my feelings ... when Boelcke suddenly appeared a few metres to my right, [and] dived down, I pulled up, yet we grazed each other and had to go back to the ground! It was only a gentle touch, but at such a furious speed it also meant a collision.'[6] Böhme, an 'old man' of 37 when he became a fighter pilot, eventually shot down 24 enemy aircraft. He remained close to Manfred von Richthofen and later commanded Jasta 2 when it was re-named 'Jasta Boelcke'. Böhme's *Pour le Mérite* award arrived on 29 November 1917, just after he had taken off on the mission in which he was shot down and killed in a fight with an Armstrong Whitworth F.K.8 two-seater.

Opposite page, top: Leutnant der Reserve Konstantin Krefft (left) scored only two victories during fifteen months with Jagdstaffel 11 and Jagdgeschwader 1, but he was one of Richthofen's most valued comrades. In October 1914, Krefft interrupted his engineering studies at Nuremberg Technical College to enlist in the Royal Bavarian Flying Service. He earned his Pilot's Badge in January 1915 and, the following month, was posted to Feldflieger-Abteilung 5b. In May, the newly promoted Vizefeldwebel [Sergeant-Major] Krefft was assigned to the single-seater unit Kampfeinsitzer-Kommando III, where he flew Fokker Eindeckers in the company of early military aviation luminaries Max Immelmann and Max Mulzer. A fearless flyer, Krefft earned the Iron Cross 2nd Class on 9 April 1915, the Bavarian Military Merit Cross 2nd Class with Swords on 17 June and the Iron Cross 1st Class in May 1916. When the latter award came, he had already been commissioned Leutnant der Reserve and assigned to Feld-

men continue to arrive at the Staffel and I am the only one of the old pupils that Richthofen still has near him. You can well imagine that he would not like to let me go right now and that at the moment I myself would not want to go. I will take my long leave later on. Richthofen gave me the full responsibility (of Staffel leadership during his absence). Hopefully I will stay in his Staffel for a long time to come.'[8] Carl Allmenröder was 21 when he was killed in combat on 27 June 1917. His elder brother had been wounded a month earlier, but survived the war and died peacefully in 1969, the day before his 75th birthday.

flieger-Abteilung 18, a 'hot' unit from which Richthofen later chose several successful fighter pilots. Krefft was transferred to Jasta 11 in October 1916 and had all the right qualifications when Richthofen was appointed to lead the unit. Krefft proved himself in battle by shooting down British aeroplanes on 11 March and 2 April 1917, but his technical skill was more highly valued by his leader and he became the Staffel's and later the Geschwader's technical/engineering officer.[7]

Right: Leutnants Wilhelm and Carl Allmenröder went to war and became pilots together. Flying two-seaters in Flieger-Abteilung (A) 227 was not fulfilling enough for the two Rhinelanders and, in November 1916, they were assigned to newly formed Jagdstaffel 11. Younger brother Carl became the more successful of the two; by the time 22-year-old Willi scored his first victory on 16 March 1917, Carl had already shot down two opponents; he got a third the following day. In five months over the Flanders Front, Carl Allmenröder was credited with 30 victories and became Jasta 11's fourth *Pour le Mérite* recipient. His last letter to his sister noted proudly the dedicated protégé's favoured position: 'Richthofen and I always fly together, each looking after the other. New

Below: Leutnant Kurt Wolff, slightly built and boyish looking, was nick-named '*zarte Blümchen*' [delicate little flower]. He was anything but delicate in combat, as he proved by shooting down 29 enemy aeroplanes during three months with Jasta 11. Wolff's score included four victories on 13 April and three on 29 April 1917, when he shot down and killed the seasoned fighter pilot Major Hubert D. Harvey-Kelly, DSO, commander of No. 19 Squadron, RFC. Orphaned as a child, Wolff found a 'family' in the German Army, first as an officer candidate in a railway regiment and then as a flyer. He succeeded Richthofen in command of Jasta 11 and his triumphs were cited by the Luftstreitkräfte's Commanding General in 1917: 'On 17 August, Jagdstaffel 11 vanquished the 200th opponent since it was first mobilised on 12 October 1916. These successes are a shining example for all fighter pilots, [and] the most beautiful memorial to the fallen comrades of Jagdstaffel 11. To the Jagdstaffel and its leader, Leutnant Wolff, [and] especially also to its former leader, Rittmeister Freiherr von Richthofen, I express my appreciation.'[9] Wolff held four Prussian bravery awards – *Pour le Mérite*, Knight's Cross with Swords of the Royal Order of the House of Hohenzollern, and the Iron Cross 2nd and 1st Classes – when he was killed in combat on 16 September 1917.

Below: Leutnant Karl-Emil Schäfer was a Richthofen protégé who learned well and went on to become a *Pour le Mérite* recipient and leader of his own Jagdstaffel. When the lessons seemed obscure, Schäfer paid attention, as he recorded after British Flights were seen forming up over their own airfields on 6 April 1917: 'We all expected that Richthofen would wait zealously until they came over, for hours if possible, right up to the last drop of fuel, as the weather was exquisite ... There was great astonishment when [his] aircraft suddenly broke into a sharp turn homeward. Perhaps he had engine trouble or had not seen the Englishmen over there. Thus, I stayed on course, as did

Royal Order of the House of Hohenzollern, which he earned while with Jasta 25. Lyncker was killed before his transfer orders came through, but Brauneck reported to Richthofen with seven confirmed victories to his credit and soon proved his worth. When Richthofen was forced down on 6 July 1917, Brauneck was one of two Jasta 11 pilots who stayed with him to ensure that he was not attacked. Five days later, acting Staffel leader Leutnant Kurt Wolff was wounded and Brauneck succeeded him in command of Jasta 11. On 22 July Brauneck wrote home: 'This morning I got my tenth. It was part of a squadron from which the Jasta under my leadership shot down three of the enemy. This afternoon the Rittmeister was here and he feels quite well.'[11] Four days later Brauneck was killed in a fight with Captain Noel W. W. Webb of No. 70 Squadron, RFC.

two others with me. But Richthofen came back, crossed right in front of us and signalled unmistakably: go home. At the airfield he called us together [and said]: "Gentlemen, there is ten minutes' time to fill up with fuel. In less than half an hour we will have a massive operation at the Front, for which I will order more and more aeroplanes. Please stay together behind them so that everything is in place when [the operation] goes off."[10] In that fight Schäfer scored the 10th and 11th of his final total of 30 victories.

Below: Leutnant Lothar Freiherr von Richthofen was a daring and successful fighter pilot in his own right but lived in his brother's shadow. Lothar, who shot down 40 enemy aeroplanes, is seen here (centre) with two other *Pour le Mérite* fighter pilots: 44-victory ace Oberleutnant Bruno Loerzer (left) and Oberleutnant Hermann Göring, victor in 22 combats and last wartime commander of the Richthofen Geschwader. While not a product of the

Above: Leutnant der Reserve Otto Brauneck came to Richthofen's attention through a mutual comrade. Oberleutnant Bodo Freiherr von Lyncker knew Richthofen from their pilot training in 1915 and wrote to seek assignment to Jasta 11 for himself and Brauneck. Both men had shot down enemy aeroplanes while flying with Jagdstaffel 25 in Macedonia and were typical of aggressive pilots hoping to fly with Germany's most successful fighter pilot. In the accompanying photograph, Brauneck wears the Knight's Cross with Swords of the

cadet system, Lothar joined the army and was commissioned into a cavalry unit and then followed Manfred into aviation: first as an observer with a bombing unit, Kampfstaffel 23 of KG 4, and then as a pilot with Jagdstaffel 11. Manfred wrote: 'Once, I saw how Lothar lagged behind a [British] flight and was attacked by an Englishman. It would have been easy for him to avoid the battle ... [but] he does not know how to run away. Luckily, I observed this and was on the alert. I watched as the Englishman, who was above him, pounced on him and opened fire. My brother tried to reach his altitude unconcerned whether he was being shot at or not. Then, all of a sudden, his machine looped and ... plunged straight down, spinning and spinning. An unexpected manoeuvre, but still a controlled dive ... With the Englishman behind him, my brother started up and in a flash was above him. The enemy aeroplane could not recover so quickly, my brother was on his neck and a few moments later flames shot out of it. Then there was nothing more to save, the other aeroplane fell down burning.'[12]

Right: Hauptmann Maximillian Sorg was 6. Armee's Officer in Charge of Aviation when Manfred von Richthofen was appointed to lead Jagdstaffel 11. Sorg was a career Army officer, beginning as a 19-year-old officer candidate in 2. Jäger-Bataillon in 1897 and changing with the times when military aviation began to show serious promise. The war was a week old when he was given command of Bavarian Feld-flieger-Abteilung 1, followed at the end of 1914 by appointment as Armee-Abteilung von Strantz's Staff Officer for Aviation. Sorg's combat flying and command experience qualified him for posting on 8 August 1916 to command all aviation units in 6. Armee's sector as the new Jagdstaffeln [fighter units] were being developed. Sorg was an able and highly decorated commander who was under-rated by Richthofen until Jasta 11 was transferred to 4. Armee's sector and placed under the authority of Hauptmann Otto Bufe. Richthofen paid a left-handed compliment to Sorg when he complained to a well-placed source in Berlin: 'I can assure you it is

no fun these days to be leader of a Jagdstaffel or in this Armee. [When I was] in the 6. Armee, after all, I had the good Sorg, who had no grasp at all of the fighter sortie and the mission of a Jagdstaffel. This Bufe is prejudiced in such a way that it is absolutely impossible to deal with him ...'[13]

Opposite page, top: Hauptmann Otto Bufe (second from left) was a decorated and promising career officer when he and Rittmeister Manfred von Richthofen began their contest of wills. Bufe, one of the top men in his class at the Main Cadet Institute, had earned regular promotions and joined the Flying Service when the war started. He advanced in command rapidly and, after leading two Feld-flieger-Abteilungen, was appointed 4. Armee's Staff Officer in Charge of Aviation on 26 September

risk that my subordinates will not agree and that it [might] cost me my position. I owe that to his memory. It is abundantly clear ... that during his lifetime no one ever talked about leadership of the Geschwader. And with me being a beginner, they will try to change that.'[15] In fact, Reinhard was very effective; he led by example with a steadily rising victory score and qualified for the *Pour le Mérite*. Like his predecessor, Reinhard attended the fighter aircraft competition at Adlershof, near Berlin. He was killed while test-flying a prototype on 3 July 1918. Wilhelm Reinhard remains connected to the Richthofen heritage, as in recent years his grave has been relocated from his hometown of Düsseldorf to Wittmund, current home of Germany's Jagdgeschwader Richthofen.

1916. When Jagdstaffel 11 was transferred to 4. Armee's sector on 10 June 1917, Bufe anticipated that he would gain greater tactical responsibilities, with the first Jagdgeschwader under his command. Instead, Jastas 4, 6, 10 and 11 were formed into JG I under Richthofen's leadership. After the Kommandeur was wounded on 6 July and was in hospital, however, Bufe took a more direct role in deploying JG I. Richthofen was angered by the changes and urged his high-ranking officer friends in Berlin to have Bufe re-assigned. Richthofen returned to JG I on 25 July and, just over a week later, Bufe was appointed 8. Armee's Officer in Charge of Aviation on the Russian Front. He resigned from the army in 1919.[14]

Right: Hauptmann Wilhelm Reinhard was Richthofen's chosen successor as commander of Jagdgeschwader I. He had only twelve victories to his credit when he succeeded his mentor on 22 April 1918, but he had been prepared for the responsibility, as he related in a letter home: 'Three days ago I was appointed Kommandeur of the Geschwader, therefore as [Richthofen's] successor. A hard task. It is good only in that he spoke with me often when he thought about his successor. I will carry out that which he told me right from his heart, [even] at the

Right: Leutnant Erich Löwen-hardt (right), like his friend, Lothar von Richthofen (left), was also born in Breslau. Löwen-hardt went off to war with Infan-terie-Regiment Nr. 141 and a month later, at the age of 17, was commissioned Leutnant. He was a brave, determined soldier and earned the Iron Cross 2nd Class and 1st Class awards on the Eastern Front. Austria–Hungary awarded him its Merit Cross 3rd Class with War Decoration for rescuing five wounded Austrian soldiers from a Russian artillery barrage. After recuperating from wounds he had received in Serbia in 1916, Löwenhardt

joined the flying service. He began as an observer with Flieger-Abteilung (A) 265 and then became a fighter pilot with Jagdstaffel 10 in March 1917. He was a tena-cious fighter and on 1 April 1918 he became leader of Jasta 10. Just over eight weeks later, with 24 victories to his credit, he was awarded the *Pour le Mérite*.[16] Following Manfred von Richthofen's death, Löwen-hardt became a surrogate brother to Lothar, who wrote that 'it was nice to be with [him], almost the way it had been with Manfred ... Since Manfred [was gone], I was happy to have again found someone on whom I could rely.'[17] But this comrade too died in combat; after colliding with Leutnant Richard Wentz on 9 August 1918, Löwenhardt bailed out, but his parachute failed to open and he died at the age of 21.

Right: Hans Klein left his studies in Berlin during the war call-up in 1914 and enlisted in an infantry regi-ment in his hometown of Stettin [today Szczecin, Poland]. During continuous service on the Western Front, he advanced in rank and, on 22 March 1915, was promoted to Leutnant der Reserve. Eleven months later he transferred to the flying service, was trained as a single-seater pilot and posted to Jagdstaffel 4, the unit with which he achieved 22

victories. Richthofen selected Klein to command Jasta 10 on 27 September 1917[18] and later wrote: 'He is one of my most successful and capable Staffel leaders. His bold gallantry, vigorous aggressive spirit and relentless daring know no bounds. As a leader in the air [he is] the very model of courage and he demands bravery of his subordinates ... His iron will-power would not allow him to be inactive at home [on recuperative leave], despite severe wounds. Scarcely recovered, he always came back to the Geschwader ahead of time.'[19] On 4 December 1917 Klein became Richthofen's seventh protégé to earn the *Pour le Mérite*.[20] He was wounded in combat on 19 February 1918 and lost his right index finger, but survived the war and went on to become a General-major in the Luftwaffe. Hans Klein died in 1944.

Above left: Leutnant Werner Voss was, Richthofen said, his 'closest competitor' in the tacit race to be Germany's top-scoring fighter pilot. But it was a friendly rivalry, the two men having known each other since their Jagdstaffel 2 days, when Voss shot down 28 enemy aeroplanes within seven months. Rapid success and an aggressive airfighting style were all they had in common; Richthofen's methodical

approach to tactics was not shared by Voss, who was five years younger and impetuous. Unhappy with one of Boelcke's successors at Jasta 2, Voss and another officer tried to have him replaced, only to find them-selves posted out of the unit. Voss was rotated through three Jasta commands – capitalising on his status as a successful airfighter and *Pour le Mérite* recipient – until Richthofen requested that he lead Jasta 10.[21] Like Richthofen, Werner Voss fell in combat over British lines on a Sunday. Alone in a Fokker Triplane on 23 September 1917, he charged into a Flight of S.E.5s from No. 56 Squadron and was shot down. Richthofen's mother followed the careers of her son's comrades and wrote about Voss: 'The audacious, reckless 20-year-old valiant young warrior, the dancing hussar who laughingly chal-lenged death ... Forty-nine times he sent down enemy aeroplanes swirling like flaming torches, then it happened to him.'[22]

Above right: Leutnant der Reserve Ernst Udet was a rising star among German fighter pilots when Richthofen recruited him for JG I in March 1918. Denied military flight instruction, Udet paid for his own flying lessons so that, on 5 June 1915, he was qualified to begin training with Flieger-Ersatz-Abteilung 9 at Darmstadt. His first posting, to Flieger-Abteilung (A) 206, ended when he was confined for a week after stunt-flying over the airfield and he then was transferred to Kampfeinsitzer-Kommando Habsheim in Alsace. During his third combat mission, on 18 March 1916, Udet shot down his first enemy aeroplane[23] and found his calling. KEK Habsheim was redesignated Jagdstaffel 15 and Udet shot down another five aeroplanes with the unit before being posted to Jasta 37 on 5 August 1917. Three months later, with his victory score at 14, he was appointed leader of Jasta 37. After going to Jasta 11, he proved his worth by shooting down three aeroplanes in two days. Richthofen gave him command of Jasta 4, with which Udet scored his 24th to 62nd victories to become Germany's second high-scoring ace of the war. He held the third-highest score of all the belligerents, following Rittmeister Manfred Freiherr von Richthofen (80), Capitaine René Fonck (75) and Lieutenant-Colonel William A. Bishop (72)[24]. A Generaloberst [Colonel-General] in the Second World War, Ernst Udet committed suicide aged 45 on 17 November 1941.[25]

Right: Leutnant Hans Joachim Wolff was Manfred von Richthofen's wingman during the Kommandeur's last combat on 21 April 1918. Nicknamed '*Wölffchen*' [wolf cub] to distinguish him from the 33-victory ace Oberleutnant Kurt Wolff, who was no relation, the younger officer had a burning ambition to follow in the footsteps of his mentor, Richthofen. Wolff was elated when his fourth victory, a Bristol F.2B which he shot down on 2 April 1918, was also recorded as Jagdstaffel 11's 250th combat success – but disappointed that he received no special recognition. To compensate him, Richthofen promised to take Wolff hunting with him at the end of the month. Instead, on that fateful third Sunday in April, Wolff was the last German to see Richthofen alive. Having finished off his seventh victim, Wolff later wrote to Lothar von Richthofen, 'I looked over at Herr Rittmeister and saw that he was at extremely low altitude over the Somme near Corbie, right behind an

Englishman. I shook my head instinctively and wondered why Herr Rittmeister was following an opponent so far on the other side. While I was still looking at where my victim had fallen, suddenly I heard a machine-gun behind me and [realised] I was being attacked by another Sopwith Camel ...'[26] Hans Joachim Wolff survived that fight, but 25 days later he was shot down and killed, ten kilometres from where his leader had fallen.

Appendix II — Jagdgeschwader Richthofen Pilot Rosters

The pilot rosters of the four Jagdstaffeln commanded by Rittmeister Manfred Freiherr von Richthofen also help to tell the Red Baron story. They show who served in which units at which times, who stayed and succeeded under the demanding Kommandeur, who died or were captured in attempting to become 'Kanonen' [aces] in these prestige-laden units, and who were 'cycled' out for not meeting Richthofen's rigorous expectations. The rosters presented here are drawn from various records and are as complete as current access to surviving German documentation allows; hence, some names and data are missing, while other information and corrected spellings are newly available.

In addition to the abbreviations noted in the introduction to this book, the following shortened forms are used here to keep this tabulation concise and functional:

AFP   Armee-Flugpark (air park for different armies, such as AFP 4 serving 4. Armee)

BG   Bombengeschwader (bomber wing, successor to Kampfgeschwader)

EoW   End of War

FA   Flieger-Abteilung (early two-seater combat units; later used for specialised missions)

FAA   Flieger-Abteilung (two-seater artillery-spotting and reconnaissance units)

FBS   Flieger Beobachter Schule (air observer training school)

FEA   Flieger-Ersatz-Abteilung (air replacement unit)

FFA   Feldflieger-Abteilung (very early two-seater combat units; forerunners of FA and FAA noted above)

FÜA   Flieger-Übungsabteilung (aviation practice unit)

Idflieg   Inspekteur der Flieger (Inspectorate of Aviation)

JG   Jagdgeschwader (fighter wing)

Js   Jagdstaffel (fighter section similar to RAF squadron)

Jssch I and Jssch II   Jagdstaffel Schulen (fighter pilot schools) I at Valenciennes and II at Nivelles

KEK and Kest   Kampfeinsitzerstaffeln (single-seat fighter units)

KG   Kampfgeschwader (combat bombing wing)

Ks   Kampfstaffel (combat bombing section)

PlM   officer received the Orden Pour le Mérite

Ss   Schutzstaffel or Schlachtstaffel (two-seater escort and ground support units)

Adding to the task of tracking German air units is that some were regional; FFA 5 was a Prussian unit and FFA 5b was provided by the Kingdom of Bavaria; the designator 's' was for Saxon units and 'w' for those from Württemberg. Finally, when lists show a pilot transferred to 'Idflieg,' it meant only that he was placed at the disposal of the aviation inspectorate for assignment elsewhere.

JAGDSTAFFEL 4

| | Victories | | From | | To | | |
	Js 4	Total	Unit	Date	Date		Unit
Commanding officers							
Oblt Hans Joachim Buddecke (PlM)	-	13	KEK Vaux	1.9.16	31.12.16		Turkey
Ltn.d.R Wilhelm Frankl (PlM)	9	19	Js 4	1.1.17	8.4.17		KiA
Oblt Kurt von Döring	10	11	FAA 227	8.4.17	6.7.17		JG I
Oblt Oskar Freiherr von Boenigk (PlM) - acting	5	26	Js 4	6.7.17	25.7.17		Js 4
Oblt Kurt von Döring			JG I	25.7.17	6.9.17		JG I
Oblt Oskar Freiherr von Boenigk - acting			Js 4	6.9.17	19.10.17		Js 21
von Oblt Kurt von Döring			JG I	23.10.17	12.12.17		JG I
Ltn.d.R Kurt Wüsthoff (PlM) - acting	27	27	Js 4	12.12.17	20.12.17		Js 4
Oblt Kurt von Döring			JG 1	20.12.17	19.1.18		JG I
Ltn.d.R Kurt Wüsthoff			Js 4	19.1.18	16.3.18		JG I
Ltn Hans-Georg von der Osten	-	5	Js 11	16.3.18	28.3.18		WiA
Ltn.d.R Johann Janzen	-	13	Js 6	28.3.18	3.5.18		Js 6
				3.5.18	21.5.18		
Ltn.d.R Ernst Udet (PlM)	39	62	Js 11	21.5.18	14.8.18		JG I
Ltn.d.R Egon Koepsch - acting	9	9	Js 4	14.8.18	19.9.18		Js 4
Oblt.d.R Ernst Udet			Leave	19.9.18	22.10.18		Leave
Ltn.d.R Heinrich Maushake	6	6	Js 4	22.10.18	3.11.18		WiA
Ltn.d.R Egon Koepsch - acting			Js 11	5.11.18	EoW		

	Victories Js 4	Total	From Unit	Date	To Date	Unit
Special Duty Officer						
Ltn.d.R Karl Meyer	3	4	Js 11	7.9.17		
Ltn.d.R Oskar Rouselle	-	-	AFP 4	16.11.17	5.9.18	AFP 4/FEA 1
Pilots						
Oblt Ernst Freiherr von Althaus (PlM)	-	9	KEK Vaux	1.9.16	4.3.17	WiA
Ltn Busso von Alvensleben	-	-		7.17	27.11.17	Js 21
Ltn.d.R Fritz Gerhard Anders	1	7	Js 35	2.6.17	18.9.17	JsSch I
					11.2.18	Js 73
Ltn.d.R Hermann Bahlmann	1	1	JsSch II	26.10.18	EoW	
Ltn Raven Freiherr von Barnekow	-	11	FEA 5	9.11.17	10.3.18	Js 20
Ltn.d.R Julius Bender	-	-	Js 10	30.5.18	16.7.18	WiA / Js 25
Ltn Fritz Otto Bernert (PlM)	4	27	KEK Vaux	1.9.16	1.3.17	Js 2
Oblt Rudolf Berthold (PlM)	4	44	KEK Vaux	1.9.16	16.10.16	Js 14
Oblt Oskar Freiherr von Boegnik	5	26	KG 6/Ks 32	24.6.17	19.10.17	Js 21
Ltn.d.R Bouillon	-	-	JG I	21.8.17		Js 10
Vzfw Ernst Clausnitzer	2	3		12.16	16.7.17	PoW
Vzfw Joseph Doerflinger	-	-	Js 10	9.9.18	10.10.18	Js 64
Ltn.d.R Heinrich Drekmann	10	11	Js 26	29.8.17	30.7.18	KiA
Ltn.d.R Martin Fischer	-	-		3.18	27.4.18	AFP 2
			JsSch I	26.8.18		Js 6
Flgr Flassbeck	-	-	JsSch II	26.10.18	EoW	
Ltn.d.R Wilhelm Frankl	9	19	KEK Vaux	1.9.16	8.4.17	KiA
Ltn.d.R Ehrhardt Fügner	-	-	KEK Vaux	1.9.16	23.9.16	WiA
			Hospital		19.5.17	KiA
Ltn.d.R Geppert	-	-	JsSch I	1.10.18	EoW	
Ltn Heinz Graf von Gluczewski-Kwilicki	2	2		12.17	EoW	
Ltn Walter Gnamm	-	-	FFA 23	1.9.16	1917	
Ltn.d.R Graul	-	-	AFP 4	3.8.17	9.17	
Ltn Gisbert-Wilhelm Groos	1	7	JsSch II	5.17	24.5.17	Js 11
Oblt Fritz Walter Grosch	-	-	JsSch I	14.8.18	12.9.18	Idflieg
Ltn Hartmann			Js 11	27.11.17	2.18	
Ltn Held			JsSch II	22.10.18	EoW	
Ltn. d. R Karl Hertz	1	3		7.9.17	26.1.18	Js 59
Ltn.d.R Adolf Hildebrandt	1	1	JsSch I	28.8.18	EoW	
Ltn.d.R Hirschfeld	-	-		7.18	28.8.18	
Ltn.d.R Walter Höhndorf (PlM)	-	12	Js 1	1.9.16	16.10.16	Js 14
Ltn.d.R Hortz	-	-	AFP 4	6.9.17		
Ltn.d.R Alfred Hübner	4	4		24.6.17	14.8.17	KiA
Ltn Fedor Hübner	2	2		30.3.18	16.5.18	PoW
Ltn.d.R Johannes Jessen	2	2		30.5.18	EoW	
Ltn.d.R Joschkowitz	1	1	JsSch I	19.9.17	1.4.18	AFP 2
Ltn.d.R Wieland Kerzmann	-		Ss 10		9.2.18	Js 58
Ltn.d.R Hans Klein (PlM)	16	22	AFP 2	22.11.16	26.8.17	AFP 4/Js 10
Ltn.d.Res Egon Koepsch	9	9	FAA 256	1.9.17		
			AFP 4	7.9.17	EoW	
Ltn.d.R Kralewski	-	-		12.16	30.10.17	Kest 8
Ltn.d.R Richard Kraut	1	1	JsSch I	3.8.18	25.10.18	Js 66
Ltn.d.R Richard Krüger	1	1		5.17	17.7.18	KiA
Ltn.d.R Krüger	-	-		24.4.18	11.5.18	AFP 2
Ltn.d.R Alfred Lenz	-	6	KEK Vaux	1.9.16	16.10.16	Js 14
Ltn Hans Malchow	1	1		1.9.16	4.17	
Ltn Wolf Baron von Manteuffel-Szöge	-	3		1.9.16	3.17	JsSch II/Js 35b
Vzfw Hermann Margot	-	-	FFA 23	1.9.16	16.10.16	Js 14
Vzfw Otto Marquardt	1	1		6.17	8.17	Js 26
Ltn Matthies	-	-		5.18	11.5.18	AFP 2
Ltn.d.R Heinrich Maushake	6	6		9.11.17	3.11.18	WiA

	Victories		From		To		
	Js 4	Total	Unit	Date	Date	Unit	
Ltn.d.R Karl Meyer	3	4	FAA 201	1.2.17	14.7.17	Js 11	
			Js 11	7.9.17	19.8.18	JsSch II	
Ltn Otto Neumüller	-	-		12.16	1.17		
Ltn.d.R Friedrich Noltenius	1	21	Js 11	4.11.18	EoW		
Vzfw Linus Patermann	2	2		.16	12.7.17	KiA	
Ltn Hans Freiherr von Puttkammer	-	1	Kest 5	30.5.18	23.7.18	AFP 7	
Ltn Viktor von Rautter gen. von Pressentin	15	15		3.18	31.5.18	KiA	
Ltn.d.R Reinhardt	1	1		22.7.18	EoW		
Flgr Kurt Rohde	-	-	JsSch II	18.8.18	EoW		
Ltn.d.R Oskar Rouselle	-		FFA 23	7.17	24.9.17	FEA 12	
			AFP 4	16.11.17	5.9.18	AFP 4 FEA 1	
Vzfw Rüldenberg (Ltn.d.R 18.9.17)	-	-					
Vzfw Karl Schmelcher	-	2	Js 18	29.4.17	5.17		
Sergt Otto Schmutzler	1	1		12.11.17	16.5.18	KiA	
Ltn Wilhelm Schulze	-	-	KEK Vaux	1.9.16	30.11.17	KiA	
Ltn.d.R Siempelkamp	1	5		2.3.18	10.4.18	AFP 2/Js 64w	
Ltn.d.R Skauradzun	-	-		12.17	8.3.18	WiA	
Ltn.d.R Spille	-	3			9.2.18	Js 58	
Ltn.d.R Karl Stehle	-	-	KEK Vaux	25.8.16	31.3.17	Kest 6	
Ltn Leo Strauch	-	-	FFA 16	11.16	9.17	Js 33	
Ltn Hans Suck	-	-	JsSch II	14.10.18	EoW		
Offstlvtr Tonnert	-	-			31.8.17	JsSch I	
Ltn Trentpohl	-	-	FFA 23	1.10.16			
Ltn.d.R Josef Veltjens (PlM)	-	37	FFA 23	10.16	11.16	Js 14	
Ltn Alfred Wenz	-	-	Js 11	20.10.18	EoW		
Ltn.d.R Wilde	1	1		9.17	2.11.17	Idflieg	
				6.4.18	Js 73		
Ltn Joachim von Winterfeld	2	2		24.4.18	5.9.18	KiA	
Ltn.d.R Kurt Wüsthoff (PlM)	27	27	KG I	6.17	16.3.18	JG I/ Js 15	
Ltn Joachim von Ziegesar	-	3	FFA 23	1.10.16	16.10.16	Js 14	
Ltn Zwitzers		-	AFP 4	23.10.17	2.18	FBS West	

JAGDSTAFFEL 6

	Victories		From		To		
	Js 6	Total	Unit	Date	Date	Unit	
Commanding Officers							
Rittm Josef Wulff	2	3	KG 5	10.9.16	1.5.17	Stofl Heimat	
Ltn Fritz Otto Bernert (PlM)	3	27	Js 2	30.4.17	9.6.17	Js 2	
Oblt Eduard Ritter von Dostler (PlM)	18	26	Js 34	10.6.17	21.8.17	KiA	
Ltn.d.L Hans Ritter von Adam (PlM)	15	21	Js 6	22.8.17	15.11.17	KiA	
Ltn.d.R Johann Czermak - acting	1	1	Kest 4a	15.11.17	26.11.17	Js 6	
Oblt Wilhelm Reinhard	6	20	Js 11	26.11.17	6.2.18	JG I	
Oblt Kurt Lischke - acting	-	-	Js 6	6.2.18	16.2.18	Js 6	
Hptm Wilhelm Reinhard			JG 1	16.2.18	22.4.18	JG I	
				22.4.18	3.5.18		
Ltn.d.R Johann Janzen	12	13	Js 4	3.5.18	9.6.18	PoW	
Ltn.d.R Hans Kirschstein (PlM)- acting	27	27	FA 3	10.6.18	16.7.18	KiC	
Ltn.d.R Paul Wenzel - acting	10	10	Js 41	19.7.18	30.8.18	Idflieg	
Ltn.d.R Ulrich Neckel (PlM)	6	30	Js 19	1.9.18	EoW		
Special Duty officer							
Oblt Kurt Lischke			FFA 39	9.7.17	EoW		
Pilots							
Ltn.d.L Hans Ritter von Adam (PlM)	18	21	Js 34b	5.7.17	15.11.17	KiA	
Vzfw Fritz Bachmann	2	2		9.17	21.10.17	KiA	
Ltn.d.R Ludwig Beckmann	-	7		12.17	21.2.18	Js 48	

	Victories		From		To	
	Js 6	Total	Unit	Date	Date	Unit
Uffz Beschow	-	2	AFP 4	23.9.17	20.4.18	AFP C
Ltn.d.R Block	-	-	JsSch I	20.9.18	EoW	
Gefr Kurt Blümener	-	-		21.7.18	8.9.18	KiA
Ltn Otto von Breiten-Landenberg	1	5		12.17	16.3.18	Js 11
				25.3.18	26.4.18	Idflieg
Ltn.d.R Moritz-Waldemar Bretschneider-Bodemer	6	6		19.4.18	18.7.18	KiA
Ltn.d.R Brocke	-	-		17.5.18	30.7.18	Idflieg
Ltn.d.R Johann Czermak	1	1	JsSch I	24.6.17	18.12.17	Js 77
Vzfw Josef Degen	-	-		17.5.18	14.6.18	PoW
Ltn.d.R Karl Deilmann	3	5	KG 5/Ks 30	10.9.16	10.9.17	AFP 4
Vzfw Eduard Ey	-	-	KEK Metz	10.9.16	18.5.17	KiC
Ltn.d.R Martin Fischer	-	-	Js 4		29.10.18	WiA
Ltn.d.R Carl Galetschky	2	3	Js 27	18.8.17	5.1.18	Js 48
Ltn.d.R Franz Götte	-	1			22.5.17	Js 20
Vzfw Häusler	1	1		3.17		
Oblt Hartmann	-	-		18.5.18	EoW	
Ltn Fritz Heidenreich	-	-		17.5.18	2.6.18	PoW
Vzfw Franz Hemer (Ltn.d.R 20.9.18)	19	19	JsSch I	10.9.17	EoW	
Vzfw Carl Holler	3	3	PFA 71	1.17	5.17	FFA 71
Ltn.d.R Johann Janzen	12	13	Js 23	16.10.17	26.3.18	Js 4
Ltn.d.R Hans Kirschstein (PlM)	27	27	JsSch 1	13.3.18	16.7.18	KiC
Ltn.d.R Wilhelm Koch	-	-	AFP 4	4.8.17	1.18	Js 55
Ltn.d.R Krayer		3	JS 10	31.7.18	13.8.18	Js 45
Vzfw Fritz Krebs	8	8		5.18	16.7.17	KiA
Vzfw Christian Kress	2	4	KEK Metz	10.9.16	10.11.16	KiA
Vzfw Heinrich Küllmer	1	3		8.5.17	2.8.17	Js 34b
Ltn.d.R Kurt Küppers	5	6		3.17	8.17	KG 3
			KG 3/Ks 14	17.11.17	16.12.17	Js 48
Vzfw Lechner	-	-		14.8.18	30.8.18	Idflieg
Ltn.d.R Fritz Loerzer	1	11	KEK Metz	10.9.16	14.2.17	Js 26
Ltn Friedrich Mallinckrodt	1	6	KEK Sivry	10.9.16	1.1.17	Js 10
Ltn Johannes Markgraf	-	-	JsSch II	11.7.18	16.7.18	KiC
Ltn.d.R Matzdorf	2	2		30.5.18	19.9.18	JsSch II
Vzfw Morzik	-	-			14.2.17	Js 26
Ltn.d.R Roland Nauck	1	1		10.16	8.4.17	KiA
Vzfw Adolf Niess	-	-		23.9.17	12.10.17	FüA Sedan
					2.18	
Ltn.d.R Werner Noldecke	-	-	JsSch I	17.6.18	22.7.18	WiA
Ltn.d.R Friedrich Noltenius	2	21	Js 27	21.9.18	20.10.18	Js 11
Vzfw Petzold	-	-			28.6.17	
Ltn.d.R Max Pollandt	-	-	Js 23	10.1.17	6.17	FAA 256
Ltn.d.R Leopold von Raffey	1	2	Js 34b	11.6.17	30.8.18	Idflieg
Ltn.d.R Erich Reiher	1	1		6.17	24.6.17	KiA
Uffz Hans Reimers	2	2		21.7.18	4.9.18	KiA
Oblt.z.S Hellmuth Riensberg	-	-	Js 10	21.10.17		Js 10
Ltn.d.R Rieth	1	1	JsSch II	11.10.18	EoW	
Ltn.d.R. Otto Rödiger	-	-	JsSch II	28.10.18	EoW	
Ltn.d.R Emil Rolff	3	3	JsSch I	2.7.18	19.8.18	KiC
Ltn Fritz Schiemann	2	2	JsSch I	15.8.18	EoW	
Ltn.d.R Julius Schmidt	-	15	FEA 6	9.9.18	EoW	
Fwltn Fritz Schubert	3	3		3.17	25.8.18	JG I
Ltn Martin Skowronski	3	3	AFP 5	24.4.18	1.7.18	AFP 3
Ltn Karl Stock	2	3	Js 22	13.7.17	5.1.18	Js 48/KiA
Ltn.d.R Walter Stock	3	3	Js 22	8.7.17	5.1.18	Js 48
Vzfw Stumpf	1	1	AFP 4	4.8.17	18.12.17	Js 77
Ltn.d.R Robert Tüxen	2	2	FAA 213	6.17	3.18	
Oblt Helmuth Volkmann	-	-		10.9.16	11.16	Js 10

	Victories		From		To		
	Js 6	Total	Unit	Date	Date		Unit
Ltn Bodo von der Wense	-	-	JsSch I	6.8.18	11.8.18		KiA
Ltn.d.R Paul Wenzel	10	10		11.8.18	30.8.18		Idflieg
Ltn.d.R Richard Wenzl	11	12	Js 11	5.18	EoW		
Ltn Ernst Wever	-	-		10.9.16	10.11.16		KiA
Ltn.d.R Wolff				1.18	20.9.18		Idflieg
Ltn.d.R Erich Zschunke				11.16	26.11.16		WiA

JAGDSTAFFEL 10

	Victories		From		To		
	Js 10	Total	Unit	Date	Date		Unit
Commanding officers							
Oblt Ludwig Karl Linck	-	-	FFA 18	21.9.16	22.10.16		KiA
Ltn.d.R Hugo Jöns - acting	-	2	Ja Sch 1	23.10.16	16.12.16		Js 17
Ltn Viktor von Fabrice - acting				11.16	11.16		
Oblt Helmuth Volkmann	-	-	Js 6	11.16	12.16		
Oblt Karl Rummelspacher - acting	-			12.16	4.17		
Ltn.d.R Albert Dossenbach (PlM)	-	-	Js 36	3.5.17	3.7.17		KiA
Oblt Ernst Freiherr von Althaus (PlM)	1	9	Js 14	6.7.17	30.7.17		JsSch II
Ltn Werner Voss (PlM)	14	48	Js 14	30.7.17	23.9.17		KiA
Oblt Ernst Weigand - acting	3	3	Js 10	24.9.17	25.9.17		KiA
Ltn.d.R Max Kühn - acting	1	3	Js 10	26.9.17	27.9.17		Js 10
Ltn.d.R Hans Klein (PlM)	6	22	Kest 1	27.9.17	19.2.18		WiA/FEA 9
Ltn.d.R Hans Weiss - acting	1	16	Js 41	27.3.18	1.4.18		Js 11
Ltn Erich Löwenhardt (PlM) - acting	54	54	Js 10	1.4.18	19.6.18		JG I
Ltn.d.R Alois Heldmann - acting	15	15	Js 10	19.6.18	6.7.18		Js 10
Oblt Erich Löwenhardt (PlM)	54	54	JG I	6.7.18	10.8.18		KiC
Ltn.d.R Alois Heldmann - acting			Js 10	10.8.18	14.8.18		Js 10
Ltn.d.R Arthur Laumann (PlM)	4	28	Js 66	14.8.18	EoW		
Special Duty Officers							
Ltn.d.R Hugo Jöns	-	2		21.9.16	16.12.16		Js 17
Oblt Hugo Schäfer	-	-		28.6.18	EoW		
Pilots							
Ltn.d.R Adomeit	-	-	JsSch I	3.8.18	21.9.18		Js 62
Offstlvtr Paul Aue	7	10		10.16	19.9.17		WiA
					31.10.17		FEA 12
			Hospital	2.18	EoW		
Ltn Bänker	-	-					
Vzfw Adam Barth (Ltn.d.R)	1	1	FFA 13	21.9.16	10.10.16		Js 11
				3.9.17			AFP 4
				30.1.18			KiA
Vzfw Bausner	-	-		7.17	7.17		
Gefr Gustav Beerendonk	-	2	KG 7/Ks 41	21.9.16	1.17		Js 20
Ltn.d.R Gustav Bellen	1	1		11.8.17	11.10.17		WiA
				23.10.17			Idflieg
				9.11.17			FEA 12
Ltn.d.R Julius Bender	-	-	JsSch I	9.5.18	30.5.18		Js 4
Ltn von Biber-Palubitzki	-	-		7.17	25.10.17		Idflieg
				9.11.17			FEA 12
Uffz Biewers	-	-		24.4.18	12.7.18		AFP 7
Ltn.d.R Gustav Boehren	-	-	JsSch I	11.9.18	18.10.18		PoW
Ltn.d.R Franz Bohlein	-	-	FAA 213	2.18	16.3.18		KiA
Ltn.d.R Walter Bordfeld	-	-		21.9.16			Js 11
Ltn.d.R Bouillon	-	-	Js 4		29.11.17		AFP 4/FAA 227
Uffz Hermann Brettel	2	4		6.17	15.8.17		WiA
					11.9.17		AFP 4
					17.9.17		Idflieg

	Victories		From		To		
	Js 10	Total	Unit	Date	Date		Unit
Vzfw Burggaler	-	-	JsSch I	10.9.17	10.4.18		AFP 2
Vzfw Cortine	-	-					
Vzfw Kurt Delang	-	2	BG 3	2.18	10.4.18		AFP 2
Ltn.d.R Friedrich Demandt	-	-		18.11.17	30.11.17		KiA
Uffz Joseph Doerflinger	-	-	JsSch I	26.8.18	9.9.18		Js 4
Uffz Hans Eissfeldt	-	-	FAA 248	28.9.16	.17		WiA
Ltn.d.R Lothar Feige	-	-		30.5.18	30.6.18		KiA
Ltn.d.R Fritz Friedrichs	21	21	JsSch I	11.1.18	15.7.18		KiA
Ltn Arthur Gilles	-	-	JsSch II	22.10.18	EoW		
Uffz Godt	-	-	FFA 24	21.9.16	10.10.16		Js 11
Ltn.d.R Julius Grassmann	10	10	FA 32	17.10.17	EoW		
Uffz Hardel	-	-		24.8.17	20.10.17		WiA
					2.11.17		Idflieg
					18.11.17		FEA 12
Offstlvtr Hebben	-	-	FFA 5	21.9.16			
Vzfw Hecht	-	-		11.17	27.12.17		PoW
Uffz Hertel	-	-		31.5.17			IiC
Vzfw Heinemann	-	1	FFA 5b	21.9.16			
Ltn.d.R Alois Heldmann	15	15	FFA 57	11.16	EoW		
Uffz Oskar Hennig	-	-	JsSch I	11.9.16	EoW		
Uffz Oskar R. Henschler	-	1	JsSch I	2.8.18	25.10.18		Js 66
Ltn.d.R Ernst Hess	-	17	Fokkerstaffel Sivry	21.9.16	12.6.17		Js 28w
Uffz Hans Howe	-	-	FFA 5	21.9.16	1.17		Js 11
Ltn.d.R Richard Kirst	-	-	JsSch II	12.10.18	5.11.18		KiA
Uffz Rudolf Klamt	-	-		12.8.18	21.8.18		WiA
			Hospital	1.10.18	EoW		
Ltn.d.R Hans Klein (PlM)	6	22	Hospital	26.4.18	EoW		
Ltn.d.R Wilhelm Kohlbach	3	5	Js 50	17.8.18	EoW		
Ltn Joachim Kortüm	-	-	Adlershof	17.3.18	10.4.18		FAA 242w
Ltn.d.R Krayer	-	1	JsSch 1	29.7.18	31.7.18		Js 6
Ltn.d.R Max Kühn	1	3		7.18	3.5-18		AFP 2
Ltn.d.R Richard Laumann	-	-		24.4.18	4.7.18		Idflieg
	-	-	Idflieg	30.7.18	8.18		
Ltn.d.R Walter Lehmann	-	-		17.6.18	1.5.18		KiA
Gefr Lemke	-	-		3.5.18			PoW
Oblt Erich Löwenhardt	54	54	FAA 265	3.17	10.8.18		KiC
Ltn.d.R Karl Maletsky	-	-	JsSch II	29.7.18	17.8.18		Js 50
Ltn Friedrich Mallinckrodt	1	6	Js 6	1.1.17	1.3.17		Js 20
Ltn Meise	-	-	JsSch II	11.10.18	EoW		
Gefr Ludwig Möller	1	1	JsSch I	10.7.18	18.7.18		KiA
Ltn Gustav Nernst	-	3	FFA 5	25.9.16	20.1.17		Js 30
Gefr Alfons Nitsche	-	-		30.3.18	12.7.18		AFP 7
Ltn Offermann	-	-	FFA 18	21.9.16	1.9.17		AFP 4
Ltn.d.R Johannes Ohlrau	1	2	FAA 252w	8.17	15.9.17		AFP 4
Uffz Oppel	-	-		5.17			
Ltn Heinrich Otto	1	1		6.5.18	6.6.18		WiA
					16.6.18		Idflieg
Vzfw Alfred Prehn	-	1	FFA 5b	21.9.16	16.11.16		Js 11
Uffz. Preiss	-	-	JG 1	6.10.17			
Ltn.d.R Rademacher	-	-		14.5.18	31.5.18		PoW
Oblt.z.S Hellmuth Riensberg	-	-	AFP 4	17.10.17	21.10.17		Js 6
					18.1.18		KiA
Ltn Max Römer	-	-	Js 14	21.9.17	2.10.17		KiA
Uffz. Rössel	-	-		8.8.17			FEA 12
Ltn.d.R Rüdenberg	-	-	JsSch 1	9.9.17	9.11.17		Idflieg
					17.11.17		FEA 5
Vzfw Schaffen	-	-	JsSch II	10.7.18	20.8.18		AFP 4

	Victories		From		To		
	Js 10	Total	Unit	Date	Date		Unit
Ltn.d.R Kurt Schibilsky	-	1	JsSch II	15.8.18	4.10.18		PoW
Flugmaat Schnell	-	-		21.9.16			
Ltn.d.R Schröder	-	-		6.5.18	7.6.18		FAA 206
Vzfw Friedrich Schumacher	5	5		3.18	4.4.18		Hospital
			Hospital	4.18	6.5.18		Idflieg
			Irdflieg	23.6.18	24.7.18		WiA
				8.8.18			Idflieg
Ltn Arthur Sienz	-	-	JsSch II	14.10.18	EoW		
Ltn Siewert							
Ltn.d.R Stoy	-	-	Js 31	31.3.18	16.6.18		Idflieg
Uffz Strecker	-	-	JsSch II	29.7.18	4.8.18		WiA
				30.8.18			Idflieg
Offstlvtr Wilhelm Viereck	-	2	KEK III	21.9.16	22.10.16		WiA
			(FFA 5b)				
Vzfw Wawzin	-	-		1.9.17	2.18		
Ltn Weber	-	-	FFA 3	21.9.16			
Oblt Ernst Weigand	3	3	AFP 4	11.7.17	25.9.17		KiA
Uffz August Werkmeister	-	-		23.9.17	25.9.17		KiA

JAGDSTAFFEL 11

	Victories		From		To		
	Js 11	Total	Unit	Date	Date		Unit
Commanding officers							
Oblt Rudolf Lang	-	-		11.10.16	14.1.17		Js 28
Ltn Manfred Freiherr von Richthofen (PlM)	64	80	Js 2	15.1.17	1.5.17		Leave
Ltn Lothar Freiherr von Richthofen (PlM) - acting	40	40	KG 4	1.5.17	13.5.17		WiA
Ltn Carl Allmenröder (PlM) - acting	30	30	Js 11	14.5.17	15.6.17		Js 11
Rittm Manfred Freiherr von Richthofen			Leave	15.6.17	26.6.17		JG I
Ltn Carl Allmenröder			Js 11	26.6.17	27.6.17		KiA
Ltn Kurt Wolff (PlM)	31	33	Js 29	28.6.17	11.7.17		WiA
Oblt Wilhelm Reinhard	14	20	Js 11	12.7.17	4.9.17		WiA
Ltn Gisbert-Wilhelm Groos - acting	6	7	Js 11	6.9.17	11.9.17		Js 11
Oblt Kurt Wolff			Hospital	11.9.17	15.9.17		KiA
Ltn Gisbert-Wilhelm Groos - acting			Js 11	16.9.17	25.9.17		Hospital
Ltn Lothar Freiherr von Richthofen			Hospital	25.9.17	19.1.18		Leave
Ltn Hans-Georg von der Osten - acting	5	5	Js 11	19.1.18	16.2.18		Js 11
Ltn Lothar Freiherr von Richthofen			Leave	16.2.18	13.3.18		WiA
Ltn Otto von Breiten-Landenberg - acting	-	5	Js 6	16.3.18	25.3.18		Js 6
Ltn.d.R Ernst Udet (PlM) - acting	3	62	Js 11	25.3.18	8.4.18		Leave
Ltn.d.R Hans Weiss - acting	5	16	Js 11	8.4.18	2.5.18		KiA
Ltn Eberhardt Mohnike - acting	8	9	Hospital	2.5.18	19.7.18		Js 11
Ltn Lothar Freiherr von Richthofen			Hospital	19.7.18	26.7.18		JG I
Oblt Erich-Rüdiger von Wedel - acting	13	13	Js 11	26.7.18	14.8.18		Js 11
Ltn Eberhardt Mohnike - acting			Js 11	14.8.18	26.8.18		Leave
Ltn Wolfram Freiherr von Richthofen - acting	8	8	Js 11	26.8.18	30.8.17		Idflieg
Oblt Erich-Rüdiger von Wedel - acting			Js 11	31.8.18	2.9.18		JG I
Ltn Eberhardt Mohnike - acting			Leave	2.9.18	4.9.18		Js 11
Oblt Erich-Rüdiger von Wedel - acting			JG I	4.9.18	8.9.18		Js 11
				8.9.17	22.10.18		JG I
Ltn.d.R Egon Koepsch	-	9	Js 11	22.10.18	4.11.18		Js 4
Oblt Erich-Rüdiger von Wedel - acting			JG I	4.11.18	Eow		
Special Duty Officers							
Ltn Karl Kleinhenz	-	-	KEK III	12.10.16	4.4.17		AFP 6
			(FFA 5b)				

	Victories Js 11	Total	From Unit	Date	To Date	Unit
Ltn Hartmann	-	-	Js 11	4.4.17	12.7.17	Js 11
Oblt Kurt Scheffer	-	-	FBS Köln	12.7.17	18.12.17	FEA 6
Ltn Karl Esser	-	-	Js 11	19.12.17	13.6.18	AFP 17
Ltn Otto Ludwig Förster	-	-		21.5.18	4.9.18	JsSch I
Ltn Gisbert-Wilhelm Gros	6	7	JG I	26.8.17	16.9.18	JsSch II
Oblt Zander	-	-		29.9.18	EoW	

Technical officer

	Victories Js 11	Total	From Unit	Date	To Date	Unit
Ltn.d.R Konstantin Krefft	2	2	KEK III (FFA 5b)	12.10.16	2.7.17	JG I

Pilots

	Victories Js 11	Total	From Unit	Date	To Date	Unit
Ltn Carl Allmenröder (PlM)	30	30	FAA 227	10.11-16	27.6.17	KiA
Ltn Wilhelm Allmenröder	1	2	Js 29	30.4.17	24.5.17	WiA
Ltn.d.R Franz Anslinger	-	3	AFP 6	11.10.16	2.3.17	Js 35
Ltn.d.R Erich Bahr	-	-	AFP 4	27.11-17	6.3.18	KiA
Vzfw Anton Baierlein	-		FFA 2	26.11.16	3.17	FEA 1b
Ltn Raven Freiherr von Barnekow	-	11	JS 4	12.17	2.18	Js 4
			JsSch I	15.8.18	23.8.18	WiA/Js 1
Flgr Adam Barth	-	2	Js 10	10.10.16		
Ltn.d.R Wilhelm Bockelmann	2	3		3.5.17	3.9.17	WiA
					15.9.17	AFP 4
Oblt Hans-Helmuth von Boddien	-	5	FA 18	6.17		
			JsSch I	17.11.17	29.1.18	Js 59
Ltn.d.R Walter Bordfeld	-	-	Js 10		18.6.17	KiA
Vzfw Georg Braumüller	-	-		16.1.17	1.3.17	AFP 6
Ltn.d.R Otto Brauneck	3	10	Js 25	10.4.17	26.7.17	KiA
Ltn Busch	-	2		26.5.17	16.7.17	Js 39
Ltn von Conta	-	-	FA 36	2.18	23.3.18	Hospital
			Hospital	4.18	29.4.18	Idflieg
			Idflieg	21.5.18	29.7.18	Hospital
			Hospital	8.18	11.9.18	FBS Jüterbog
Ltn.d.R von Dorrien	-	-	JsSch I	2.7.18	25.7.18	WiA
			Hospital	14.9.18	10.10.18	FEA 5
Uffz Robert Eiserbeck	-	-		4.18	12.4.18	KiA
Ltn Karl Esser	-	-		1.17	13.6.18	AFP 17
Ltn.d.R Max Festler	-	-	JsSch II	26.7.18	11.8.18	KiA
Vzfw Sebastian Festner	12	12	FEA 1b	10.10.16	23.4.17	KiA
Vzfw Willi Gabriel	10	11	Ss 15	17.4.18	20.7.18	Leave
			Leave	20.8.18	22.8.18	AFP 2
Ltn Alfred Gerstenberg	-	-	KG 2	16.9.17	20.10.17	WiA
					5.11.17	FEA 11
Uffz Godt	-	-	Js 10	10.10.16		
Ltn Gisbert-Wilhelm Groos	-	-	Js 4	24.5.17	14.9.17	WiA
					15.10.17	JsSch II
Ltn.d.R Siegfried Gussmann	4	5	FA 3	29.10.17	26.4.18	Idflieg
			FEA 5	22.8.18	EoW	
Ltn Hartmann	-	-	KEK Jametz	12.10.16	27.11.17	Js 4
Ltn Hintmann	-	-		12.10.16	5.17	
Ltn.d.R Hans Hintsch	2	3		12.10.16	25.5.17	KiA
Ltn Friedrich Hoffmann	-	-		30.5.18	30.6.18	KiA
Ltn Friedrich Franz Graf von Hohenau	-	-		26.6.18	25.7.18	WiA
					26.7.18	DoW
Vzfw Otto Heller	-	-		8.4.17	15.5.17	FAA 238
Sergt Hans Howe	-	-	Js 10	11.10.16	17.2.17	AFP 6
Vzfw Jagla	-	-		11.5.18	29.7.18	AFP 7

	Victories		From		To		
	Js 11	Total	Unit	Date	Date		Unit
Ltn.d.R Erich Just	6	6	JsSch I	19.9.17	3.3.18		WiA
			Hospital	7.18	EoW		
Oblt Walther Karjus	-	-	FAA 227	26.3.18	29.5.18		AFP 2
Ltn Keseling	-	-		2.18	24.3.18		PoW
Ltn.d.R Friedrich August Freiherr von Köckeritz	3	3	JsSch I	30.7.18	EoW		
Ltn.d.R Egon Koepsch	-	9	Js 4	20.10.18	4.11.18		Js 4
Vzfw Josef Lautenschlager	1	1		14.5.17	29.10.17		KiA
Ltn Hans Karl von Linsingen	-	-	KG 2	27.11.17	24.1.18		IiC
					26.2.18		Ja 59
Ltn Friedrich-Wilhelm Lübbert	-	-	FA 18	12.17	17.2.18		WiA
Ltn Hans-Georg Eduard Lübbert	-	-		11.16	30.3.17		KiA
Ltn.d.R Otto Maashoff	3	3	FA 5	28.4.17	3.9.17		Kest 2
Vzfw Arthur Martens	-	-	JsSch I	6.8.18	10.10.18		Js 64
Ltn Matthof	-	-		12.10.16	2.17		
Ltn.d.R Karl Meyer	2	4	FAA 201	14.7.17	6.9.17		Js 4
Ltn Eberhardt Mohnike	8	9		30.4.17	1.3.18		WiA
			Hospital	11.5.18	26.8.18		Leave
			Leave	2.9.18	8.9.18		Idflieg
Ltn.d.R Franz Müller	2	2	FA 18	15.7.17	27.10.17		KiA
Ltn.d.R Alfred Niederhoff	5	7	Js 20	30.4.17	28.7.17		KiA
Vzfw Alfred Niemz	2	4	JsSch II	30.9.18	EoW		
Ltn.d.R Friedrich Noltenius	5	21	Js 6	20.10.18	4.11.18		Js 6
Ltn Albert Oesterreicher	-	-	KEK III (FFA 5b)	12.10.16	16.3.17		
Ltn Hans-Georg von der Osten	5	5	JsSch I	11.8.17	24.10.17		Leave
			Leave	3.11.17	16.3.18		Js 4
Ltn Günther Pastor	-	1	FEA 14	22.9.17	31.10.17		KiA
Ltn Wolfgang Plüschow	-	1		12.10.16	20.5.17		
Vzfw Alfred Prehn	-	1	Js 10	16.10.16	1.3.17		Navy
Ltn von Raczek	-	-	JsSch II	18.8.18	EoW		
Oblt Wilhelm Reinhard	14	20	FA 28	1.5.17	15.9.17		AFP 4
					26.11.17		Js 6
Ltn Lothar Freiherr von Richthofen (PlM)	40	40	KG 5/Ks 25	6.3.17	13.5.17		WiA
			Hospital	25.9.17	13.3.18		WiA
			Hospital	19.7.18	13.8.18		WiA
Ltn Karl-Emil Schäfer (PlM)	22	30	KG 2/Ks 11	5.2.17	26.4.17		Js 28
Ltn Carl August von Schönebeck	3	8	FAA 203	1.6.17	26.1.18		Js 59
Vzfw Edgar Scholz (Ltn.d.R 2.5.18)	5	6	KG 2/Ks 10	1.18	2.5.18		KiA
Ltn.d.R Julius Schulte-Frohlinde	4	4	JsSch I	28.8.18	EoW		
Ltn Traugott von Schweinitz	-	-		27.11.17	27.12.17		KiA
Ltn Georg Simon	1	1		7.11.16	29.1.17		WiA
			Hospital	13.3.17	4.6.17		PoW
Ltn Eberhardt Stapenhorst	4	4	AFP 4	30.6.17	13.1.18		PoW
Ltn Werner Steinhäuser	9	10	FAA 261	9.11.17	17.3.18		WiA
			Hospital	2.4.18	26.6.18		KiA
Ltn.d.R Ernst Udet (PlM)	3	62	Js 37	18.3.18	8.4.18		Hospital
Oblt Erich-Rüdiger von Wedel	13	13		23.4.18	Eow		
Ltn.d.R Hans Weiss	5	16	Js 10	1.4.18	2.5.18		KiA
Ltn Alfred Wenz	-	-	JsSch I	26.7.18	20.10.18		Js 4
Ltn.d.R Richard Wenzl	-	11	Js 31	27.3.18	17.5.18		Js 6
Ltn Hans Joachim Wolff	10	10	FAA 216w	6.7.17	14.8.17		WiA
			Hospital	11.17	16.5.18		KiA
Ltn Kurt Wolff	31	33	KG	12.10.16	11.7.17		WiA
			Hospital		2.5.17		Js 29

Notes

Foreword

1   *Algemeen Handelsblad* No. 28786,
    13 May 1917, p. 1 translated as 'Der
    Bericht eines Holländers' in
    Malkowsky, E. (ed.). *Vom
    Heldenkampf der deutschen
    Flieger,* p. 93.
    Grosz, P. and Schneide, K. 'Histori-
    ography: Cockburn-Lange' in *WW I
    Aero*, 1984, pp. 4–13.

Chapter 1

1. O'Connor, N. *Aviation Awards of
    Imperial Germany in World War I*,
    vol. II, pp. 238–9.
2. Grosz, P. 'The Agile and Aggressive
    Albatros' in *Air Enthusiast Quar-
    terly*, No. 1, 1976, p. 37.
3. Garwood, J. 'The Survivors' in *Cross
    & Cockade Journal*, 1961, pp. 368–9.
4. Richthofen, Manfred von. *Der rote
    Kampfflieger* (1917 edn.), p. 10.
5. Ibid., pp. 12–13.
6. Ibid., p. 14.
7. An officer in Dragoner-Regiment Nr.
    8; ref: Perthes, J. *Ehrentafel der
    Kriegsopfer des reichsdeutschen
    Adels 1914–1919*, p. 199.
8. An officer with Dragoner-Regiment
    Nr. 7; ref: ibid., p. 68.
9. Richthofen, op. cit., p. 44.
10. Ibid., p. 45.
11. Ibid., pp. 45–6.
12. Ibid., p. 48.
13. Idflieg, *Jagdgeschwader I
    Erfahrungsaustausch*, pp. 12–13.
14. Richthofen, op. cit., p. 58.
15. Ibid., p. 60.
16. Ibid., p. 65.
17. Ibid., p. 66.
18. *Für Tapferkeit und Verdienst*,
    Munich, 1956, p. 28.
19. Ibid.
20. Richthofen, op. cit., pp. 67–8.
21. Ibid., pp. 72–3. Richthofen wrote

this passage while at home on leave
following his 52nd combat success
and meeting with Kaiser Wilhelm II;
hence, this reference reflected his
score as of early May 1917.
22. Ibid., p. 79.
23. Ibid., pp. 79-80.
24. Quoted in Richthofen, Manfred von.
    Ein Heldenleben, p. 189.
25. Immelmann, M. *Meine Kampfflüge*,
    pp. 79–80; Immelmann's victims
    were 2/Lt John Gay, aged 22 (DoW),
    and Lt David Leeson (PoW).
26. Ibid., pp. 189–90.
27. *Der rote Kampfflieger*, op. cit.,
    p. 81.
28. Böhme, E. *Briefe eines deutschen
    Kampffliegers an ein junges
    Mädchen*, p. 41.
29. Richthofen, op. cit., pp. 83, 85.
30. Ibid., p. 88.
31. O'Connor, op. cit., p. 219.

Chapter 2

1. Boelcke, O. *Hauptmann Boelckes
    Feldberichte*, pp. 111–12; Airco
    D.H.2 7895 of No. 32 Squadron,
    Capt R. E. Wilson (PoW); early
    encounters with Vickers F.B.5
    'pusher' biplanes led German pilots
    to identify similar-appearing craft as
    'Vickers' or 'Vikkers' types.
2. Ibid., pp. 113–14; Sopwith 1½-
    Strutter A.9897 of No. 70 Squadron,
    2/Lt John H. Gale, aged 19, and Cpl
    Jeffrey M. Strathy, aged 24 (both
    KiA); D.H.2 7873 of No. 24
    Squadron, 2/Lt J. V. Bowring of No.
    24 Squadron (WiA/PoW).
3. Quoted in Richthofen, *Ein Helden-
    leben*, pp. 190–1; F.E.2b 7018 of No.
    11 Squadron, 2/Lt Lionel B. F.
    Morris, aged 19, and Capt Thomas
    Rees, aged 21 (both DoW); Ltn von
    Schweinichen, aged 23 and an
    officer in 1. Garde-Dragoner-Regi-

ment, was killed at Maurepas on 24
August 1916.
4. Boelcke, op. cit., p. 53
5. Radloff, B. and Niemann, R. 'The
    Ehrenbechers – Where Are They
    Now?' in *Cross & Cockade Journal*,
    1969, p. 366.
6. Hook, J. 'A Visit to the Richthofen
    Museum' in *Popular Flying*, 1934,
    p. 535.
7. *Ein Heldenleben*, op. cit., pp.
    191–2; F.E.2b 6973 of No. 11
    Squadron, Lt Ernest C. Lansdale,
    aged 21, and Sgt Albert Clarkson,
    aged 22 (both KiA).
8. Stofl 1. Armee *Wochenbericht*, 9
    October 1916, p. 4.
9. Hobson, C. *Airmen Died in the
    Great War 1914–1918*, p. 45.
10. *Ein Heldenleben*, op. cit., pp. 171–2.
11. Richthofen, M. von. *Der rote
    Kampfflieger* (1917 edn.), p. 96.
12. *Ein Heldenleben*, op. cit.,
    pp. 192–3.
13. Ibid., p. 77.
14. Ibid., p. 193.
15. G. G. 'Führende Männer im
    Weltkrieg – Fliegerhauptmann
    Boelcke' in *Kriegs-Echo*, Nr. 118,
    1916, p. 93.
16. Richthofen, op. cit., pp. 101–2.
17. Ibid., pp. 104–5.
18. Ibid., pp. 106–7.
19. Ibid., pp. 108–9.
20. Ibid.
21. B.E.2d 67432 of No. 16 Squadron,
    Lt Percival W. Murray, aged 20, and
    Lt Duncan J. McRae, aged 24 (both
    DoW).
22. Schäfer, K. *Vom Jäger zum Flieger*,
    pp. 81–2; Sopwith 1½-Strutter
    A.1109 of No. 43 Squadron, 2/Lt
    Philip L. Wood and 2/Lt Alan H.
    Fenton, aged 23 (both KiA).
23. No. 40 Squadron Combat Report, 9
    March 1917, 2/Lt H. C. Todd in
    F.E.8 6425.

24. Richthofen, op. cit., pp. 114–15.
25. Ibid., pp. 170–1.
26. *Ein Heldenleben*, op. cit., pp. 205–6.
27. Ferko, A. E. *Richthofen*, p. 15.
28. *Ein Heldenleben*, op. cit., p. 222.
29. Kofl 6. Armee *Wochenbericht* Nr. 25000, 30 March 1917, p. 3 notes: 'Am 23.3.17 wurde der Führer von J.St. 11 Frhr. v.Richthofen durch A.K.O. ausser der Reihe zum Oberleutnant befördert.'
30. Quoted in *Ein Heldenleben*, op. cit., p. 195.
31. Royal Flying Corps *Communiqué* No. 80, 25 March 1917, p. 1.
32. Perthes, J. *Ehrentafel der Kriegsopfer des reichsdeutschen adels 1914–1919*, Gotha, 1921, p. 185.
33. Richthofen Combat Reports, PRO.

Chapter 3

1. Richthofen, M. von. *Der rote Kampfflieger* (1917 edn.) pp. 1223; B.E.2d 5841 of No. 13 Squadron, Lt Patrick J. G. Powell, aged 21, and 1/AM Percy Bonner, aged 23 (both KiA).
2. Ibid., pp. 1256; Sopwith 1½-Strutter A.2401 of No. 43 Squadron, 2/Lt Algernon P. Warren, aged 19 (PoW), and Sgt Reuel Dunn, aged 24 (KiA).
3. Ibid., p. 126; Richthofen's combat report indicates that the Observer, who later died of his wounds, fought until the end; hence the uninjured pilot most likely continued to fight from the ground.
4. Bruce, J. *British Aeroplanes 1914–1918*, p. 128.
5. Richthofen Combat Reports, PRO; Richthofen's 35th and 36th victims were: F.2A A.3343, Lt Alfred T. Adams, aged 20 (PoW), and Lt Donald J. Stewart, (WiA/PoW); and F.2A A.3340, 2/Lt Arthur N. Lechler, aged 27 (WiA/PoW), and Lt Herbert D. K. George, aged 19 (DoW).
6. Burge, C. *The Annals of 100 Squadron*, p. 67; F.E.2b 7669 of No. 100 Squadron, 2/Lt L. Butler and 2/AM D. Robb (both PoW).
7. Royal Flying Corps *Communiqué* No. 82, 8 April 1917, p. 4.
8. Richthofen, op. cit., pp. 134–5.
9. Richthofen Combat Reports, PRO; Nieuport A.6645 of No. 60 Squadron, 2/Lt George O. Smart, aged 31 (KiA).
10. Schäfer, K. *Vom Jäger zum Flieger*, p. 103.
11. Quoted in Gibbons, F. *The Red Knight of Germany*, pp. 200–01.
12. RFC *Western Front Casualty List*, 16 April 1917.
13. O'Connor, N. *Aviation Awards of Imperial Germany in World War I*, vol. II, p. 109.
14. Zuerl, W. *Pour le Mérite-Flieger*, p. 431.
15. Quoted in Richthofen, M. von. *Ein Heldenleben*, pp. 301–2.
16. Ibid., pp. 306–7.
17. Morris, A. *Bloody April*, p. 15.
18. Quoted in *Ein Heldenleben*, op. cit., pp. 162–3.
19. Richthofen, op. cit., pp. 63–4.
20. Quoted in *Ein Heldenleben*, op. cit., pp. 318–19.
21. RFC *Western Front Casualty List*.
22. Ferko, A. E. *Richthofen*, p. 22.
23. Quoted in *Ein Heldenleben*, op. cit., pp.332–3.
24. Hobson, C. *Airmen Died in the Great War 1914–1918*, p. 39.
25. Ferko, op. cit., pp. 19, 79.
26. No. 25 Squadron Combat Report of Capt C. H. C. Woolervan, 2/Lt R. G. Malcom, Lt G. S. French, 2/Lt S. King, Sgt R. Mann, Lt R. J. Stubbington, Sgt J. H. Brown, Sgt L. Emsden, Lt G. P. Harding, Sgt H. G. Taylor, L/Cpl J. Dillon and Tpr J. Lawrence in F.E.2bs 7003, 4839, A.815, A.782, A.5522 and A.5505; Lts French and Harding in F.E.2b A.815 (both PoW); Lt Harding escaped and arrived in the UK on 22 October 1917 (ref: RFC *Western Front Casualty List*).
27. Hoeppner, E. von. *Deutschlands Krieg in der Luft*, p. 104.
28. Schäfer, op. cit., p. 111.
29. O'Connor, op. cit., p. 219.
30. SPAD S.7 B.1573 and SPAD S.7 A.6681 of No. 19 Squadron, 2/Lt Richard Applin, aged 22, and Major Hubert D. Harvey-Kelly, DSO, aged 26 (both KiA).
31. Quoted in *Ein Heldenleben*, op. cit., p. 212.
32. B.E.2e 7092 of No. 12 Squadron, 2/Lt John H. Westlake, aged 19 (DoW 7 May 1917), and 2/Lt Cyril J. Pile, aged 19 (KiA).
33. B.E.2c 2738 of No. 12 Squadron, 2/Lt David E. Davies, aged 25, and 2/Lt George H. Rathbone, aged 21 (both KiA); RFC *Western Front Casualty List* and other sources describe the aircraft as a B.E.2e, but the serial number 2738 was applied to an earlier 2c model (ref: Bruce, J. *British Aeroplanes 1914–1918*, p. 371).
34. Richthofen, op. cit., p. 150.
35. Ibid., pp. 151–2; Sopwith Triplane N.5463 of No. 8 Squadron, RNAS, F/S/Lt Albert E. Cuzner, aged 27 (KiA).
36. Ibid., pp. 154–5.

Chapter 4

1. Richthofen, M. von. *Der rote Kampfflieger* (1917 edn.), p. 155.
2. Ibid., pp. 157, 158–9.
3. Ibid., p. 159.
4. Quoted in *Ein Heldenleben*, p. 223.
5. Salzmann, E. von. 'Führende Männer im Weltkrieg – Erich von Falkenhayn' in *Kriegs-Echo*, Nr. 75, 1916, p. 13.
6. Kaiser Alexander Garde-Regiment Nr. 1 in Berlin; Supf, P., *Das Buch der deutschen Fluggeschichte*, vol. II, p. 290.
7. Quoted in Lampel, P. *Als Gast beim Rittmeister Freiherr von Richthofen*, p. 219.
8. Idflieg, *Jagdgeschwader I Erfahrungsaustausch*, p. 11.
9. Stofl 6. Armee *Wochenbericht* Nr. 19003, Teil 9, 2 October 1916.
10. Baron, G. *Schlesische Flieger Nachrichten*, p. 3; born on 6 December 1884 in Glatz, Silesia, Otto Zimmer-Vorhaus had a distinguished career in German aviation industry management until a political dispute in 1936 led to his leaving the Heinkel Company. Taken prisoner in Berlin at the end of the Second World War, he died in Russian captivity at Breslau-Hundsfeld on 31 December 1945.
11. Idflieg, op. cit., p. 8.
12. Richthofen, K. von. *Mein Kriegstagebuch*, p. 106.

13. Richthofen, M. von. *Der rote Kampfflieger* (1933 edn.), p. 176.
14. Quoted in *Ein Heldenleben*, op. cit., p. 196.
15. Zuerl, W. *Pour le Mérite-Flieger*, pp. 495–8; Nieuport 17 A.6615 of No. 1 Squadron, 2/Lt Hugh Welch, aged 20 (KiA).
16. O'Connor, N. *Aviation Awards of Imperial Germany in World War I*, vol. II, p. 91.
17. *Mein Kriegstagebuch*, op. cit., pp. 108–9.
18. Ibid., pp. 108–9.
19. Ibid., p. 112.
20. Shores, C., et al., *Above the Trenches*, p. 102.
21. Robertson, B. *British Military Aircraft Serials 1911–1971*, p. 85; Simon's Albatros D.III 2015/16 received the engine from G 39, Jasta 2 Albatros D.III 796/17, brought down on 19 May 1917.
22. Quoted in *Ein Heldenleben*, p. 197.
23. Quoted in ibid., p. 333.
24. Quoted in ibid., pp. 196–7.
25. Grosz, P. 'Agile and Aggressive Albatros' in *Air Enthusiast*, No. 1, 1976, pp. 46–7.
26. Quoted in Kilduff, P. *Richthofen – Beyond the Legend of the Red Baron*, p. 137.
27. Hoeppner, E. von. *Deutschlands Krieg in der Luft*, p. 115.
28. Bodenschatz, K. *Jagd in Flanderns Himmel*, p. 148.
29. *Kriegs-Echo*, Nr. 152, 13 July 1917, p. 664.
30. D.H.4 A.7473 of No. 57 Squadron, Capt Norman G. NcNaughton, aged 27, and Lt Angus H. Mearns, aged 22 (both KiA).
31. Quoted in *Ein Heldenleben*, op. cit., p. 167.
32. On 25 June 1917, R.E.8 A.3847, Lt Leslie S. Bowman, aged 20, and 2/Lt James E. Power-Clutterbuck, aged 23 (both KiA); and on 2 July 1917, R.E.8 A.3538, Sgt Hubert A. Whatley, aged 19, and 2/Lt Frank G. B. Pascoe, aged 20 (both KiA).
33. Quoted in *Ein Heldenleben*, op. cit., p. 163.
34. Bodenschatz, op. cit., p. 16.
35. Ibid.
36. Quoted in *Ein Heldenleben*, op. cit., pp. 147–8.

37. Feldlazarett Nr. 76 zu Kortrik, Hauptkrankenbuch Nr. 286, 25 July 1917.
38. Ibid.
39. Bodenschatz, op. cit., p. 23.

Chapter 5

1. On 16 July 1917 Vizefeldwebel Ernst Clausnitzer of Jagdstaffel 4 was forced down within British lines and captured. Comments from his interrogation noted only that the 'prisoner states that Rittmeister von Richthofen commands a group of Jagdstaffeln' and made no mention of Richthofen's condition (Ref. RFC, *Periodical Summary of Aeronautical Information*, No. 10, 23 July 1917, p. 2).
2. Kogenluft, *Nachrichtenblatt der Luftstreitkräfte*, Nr. 20, 12 July 1917, p. 70.
3. Kofl 4. Armee, *Meldung*, Nr. 24406/19, 13 July 1917, p. 7.
4. Quoted in Richthofen, M. von. *Ein Heldenleben*, p. 151.
5. RFC, *No. 32 Squadron Record Book*, 11 July 1917, p. 233.
6. Quoted in Bodenschatz, K. *Jagd in Flanderns Himmel*, p. 25.
7. Bodenschatz, op. cit., pp. 30–1.
8. Ibid., p. 36.
9. Osten, H-G. von der. 'Memoirs of World War I with Jagdstaffeln 11 and 4', in *Cross & Cockade Journal*, 1974, p. 221.
10. Quoted in Bodenschatz, op. cit., p. 38; Nieuport 23 A.6611 of No. 29 Squadron, 2/Lt William H. T. Williams, aged 19 (KiA).
11. No. 29 Squadron Combat Report No. 75, 16 August 1917, 2/Lt J. D. Payne in Nieuport B.1602.
12. Osten, H-G. von der, op. cit.
13. Quoted in Bodenschatz, op. cit., p. 40.
14. Haythornthwaite, P. *World War One Source Book*, p. 338.
15. Bodenschatz, op. cit., p. 41.
16. Grosz, P., and Ferko, A. E. 'Fokker Dr.I – Re-appraisal', in *Air Enthusiast*, No, 8, 1978, p. 18.
17. Bodenschatz, op. cit., p. 154.
18. Zuerl, W. *Pour le Mérite-Flieger*, p. 362.
19. RFC, *Communiqué*, No. 102, 26 August 1917, p. 7; one month later Lt Sharples was shot down and

killed by ground fire.
20. Quoted in Salzmann, E. von. 'Führende Männer im Weltkrieg – General d.I. Sixt von Armin' in *Kriegs-Echo*, Nr. 185, p. 1164.
21. Quoted in Bodenschatz, op. cit., p. 42.
22. SPAD S.7 B.3492 of No. 19 Squadron, 2/Lt Coningsby P. Williams (KiA).
23. Quoted in *Ein Heldenleben*, op. cit., p. 198.
24. Bodenschatz, op. cit., p. 155.
25. 'Führende Männer im Weltkrieg – General von Lossberg' in *Kriegs-Echo*, Nr 166, p. 860.
26. Bodenschatz, op. cit., p. 33.
27. W. H. 'Führende Männer im Weltkrieg – Reichskanzler Dr. Michaelis' in *Kriegs-Echo*, Nr. 155, p. 686.
28. Ibid., p. 685.
29. Bodenschatz, op. cit., p, 43; R.E.8 B.782 of No. 6 Squadron, 2/Lt John C. B. Madge, aged 25 (PoW), and 2/Lt Walter Kember, aged 26 (KiA).
30. Ibid.
31. Quoted in ibid., p. 43.
32. Ibid., pp. 43, 155; Sopwith Pup B.1754 of No. 46 Squadron, Lt Kenneth W. McDonald, aged 21 (DoW).
33. No. 46 Squadron Record Book entry for 3 September 1917.
34. Bodenschatz, op. cit., pp. 44, 156.
35. Quoted in *Ein Heldenleben*, op. cit., pp. 330–1.
36. Richthofen, K. von. *Mein Kriegstagebuch*, pp. 127–8.
37. Ibid., p. 128.
38. Ibid., pp. 128–9.
39. Quoted in *Ein Heldenleben*, op. cit., p. 334.
40. Quoted in Gibbons, F. *The Red Knight of Germany*, p. 108.
41. *Ein Heldenleben*, op. cit., pp. 152–4.
42. Richthofen, M. von. *Der rote Kampfflieger* (1933 edn.), pp. 201–2.

Chapter 6

1. Zuerl, W. *Pour le Mérite-Flieger*, pp. 274–5.
2. *Nachrichtenblatt der Luftstreitkräfte*, Nr. 36, 1 November 1917, p. 351.

3. Bodenschatz, K., *Jagd in Flanderns Himmel*, pp. 54–5.
4. Zuerl, op. cit., pp. 203–4.
5. Bodenschatz, op. cit., pp. 55, 162.
6. *Nachrichtenblatt*, Nr. 43, 20 December 1917, p. 469.
7. Henshaw, T., *The Sky Their Battlefield*, pp. 255–6.
8. Jones, H. A. *The War in the Air*, vol. IV, pp. 2467.
9. Franks, N., et al., *Under the Guns of the Red Baron*, p. 160.
10. Osten, H-G. von der. 'Memoirs of World War I with Jagdstaffeln 11 and 4', in *Cross & Cockade Journal*, 1974, p. 223.
11. Bodenschatz, op. cit., p. 57; S.E.5a B.644 of No. 41 Squadron, Lt Donald A. D. I. MacGregor, aged 22 (KiA).
12. von der Osten, op. cit.; D.H.5 A.9509 of No. 24 Squadron, 2/Lt Ian D. Campbell (KiA).
13. Quoted in Richthofen, M. von. *Ein Heldenleben*, p. 312.
14. Ibid., p. 313.
15. Bodenschatz, op. cit., pp. 58–9.
16. Quoted in *Ein Heldenleben*, op. cit., pp. 318–19.
17. Bodenschatz, op. cit., p. 166.
18. Ibid., p. 63.
19. Ibid., pp. 159–60.
20. Van Ishoven, A. *The Fall of an Eagle*, pp. 54–5.
21. Osten, von der, op. cit., p. 224.
22. Grosz, P., and Ferko, A. E. 'Fokker Dr.I Reappraisal,' in *Air Enthusiast*, No. 8, 1978, pp. 21–3.
23. Bodenschatz, op. cit., p 168.
24. *Ein Heldenleben*, op. cit., p. 200.
25. RFC, *War Diary*, 13 January 1917, p. 37.
26. Quoted in Bodenschatz, op. cit., pp. 60–1.
27. Nowarra, H., and Brown, K. *Von Richthofen and the Flying Circus*, p. 143.
28. RFC, *Summary of Air Intelligence*, No. 17, 1 March 1918.
29. Bodenschatz, op. cit., p. 169.
30. Quoted in *Ein Heldenleben*, op. cit., p. 230.
31. Osten, von der, op. cit.
32. No. 48 Squadron Combat Report No. 477 of 2/Lt H. H. Hartley and Lt J. H. Robertson in F.2B A.7114.
33. Henshaw, op. cit., p. 279.

34. RFC, *Western Front Casualty List*, 14 March 1918.
35. Public Record Office, Richthofen Combat Reports; F.2B B.1251 of No. 62 Squadron, 2/Lt Leonard C. F. Clutterbuck and 2/Lt Henry J. Sparks, aged 27 (both PoW).
36. All Bristol F.2Bs from No. 62 Squadron, RFC: B.1247, Capt Douglas S. Kennedy, MC, aged 30, and Lt Hugh G. Gill, aged 28 (both KiA); B.1250, 2/Lt C. B. Fenton and Lt H. B. P. Boyce (both PoW); and C.4824, Lt J. A. A. Ferguson and Sgt L. S. D. Long (both PoW).
37. Quoted in Bailey, Duiven and Manning, 'A Short History of No. 62 Squadron, RFC/RAF', in *Cross & Cockade Journal*, 1976, pp. 292–3.
38. RFC, *Communiqué*, No. 131, 20 March 1918, p. 3.
39. Quoted in *Ein Heldenleben*, op. cit., pp. 215–16.
40. Sopwith F.1 Camel B.5590 of No. 73 Squadron, Lt Elmer E. Heath (WiA/PoW).
41. No. 73 Squadron Combat Report No. 13 of Capt A. H. Orlebar in Sopwith Camel B.7282.
42. Udet, E., *Mein Fliegerleben*, pp. 65–6.
43. Flashar, R. 'In der Tankschlacht von Cambrai', in *In der Luft unbesiegt*, pp. 96–7.
44. Udet, op. cit., p. 66.
45. Bristol F.2B C.4844 of No. 11 Squadron, Capt Alan P. Maclean, aged 22 (DoW), and Lt Frederick H. Cantlon, MC, aged 24 (KiA).
46. Not credited to Richthofen or Löwenhardt, but most likely Airco D.H.4 A.7587 of No. 5 Squadron, RNAS, F/S/Lt C. E. Wodehouse (WiA) and AGL L. James; crew made it back to British lines (Ref. Bartlett, C. *Bomber Pilot 1916–1918*, p. 143).
47. Sopwith F.1 Camel B.5243 of No. 54 Squadron, 2/Lt William G. Ivamy, aged 28 (PoW).
48. Bodenschatz, op. cit., p. 70; the order was dated 10 March and was given to Geschwader-Adjutant Bodenschatz three days later.
49. Reinhard, W. *Personal-Bogen*, 1918.
50. Quoted in Zuerl, op. cit., p. 535.

Chapter 7

1. Quoted in Richthofen, K von. *Ein Heldenleben*, p. 229.
2. Quoted in Bodenschatz, K. *Jagd in Flanderns Himmel*, p. 74; S.E.5a C.1054 of No. 41 Squadron, Lt John P. McCone, aged 27 (KiA).
3. Bodenschatz, op. cit., pp. 75–6.
4. Udet, E. *Mein Fliegerleben*, pp. 72–3.
5. Quoted in Nowarra, H., 'A Bomber Chief and a Fighter Pilot – Two Interviews' in *Cross & Cockade Journal*, 1960, pp. 60–1.
6. *Nachrichtenblatt der Luftstreitkräfte*, Nr. 6, 4 April 1918, pp. 80–1.
7. R.E.8 A.3868 of No. 52 Squadron, Lieutenant Ernest D. Jones, aged 19, and 2/Lt Robert F. Newton (both KiA).
8. Quoted in Lampel, P. 'Als Gast beim Rittmeister Frhr. v. Richthofen', in Neumann, G. (ed.). *In der Luft unbesiegt*, p. 215.
9. Sopwith F.1 Camel D.6491 of No. 46 Squadron, Capt Sidney P. Smith, aged 21 (KiA).
10. Quoted in *Ein Heldenleben*, op. cit., p. 319.
11. Wenzl, R. *Richthofen-Flieger*, p. 18.
12. Possibly the Fokker Dr.I flown by Jasta 11 pilot Ltn.d.R Siegfried Gussmann, who was wounded in that fight and forced to return to Léchelle (Ref: Bodenschatz, op. cit., p. 176).
13. No. 73 Squadron Combat Report, 7 April 1918, 2/Lt R. R. Rowe in Sopwith F.1 Camel D.1655.
14. 2/Lt A. V. Gallie in Sopwith F. 1 Camel D.6550 of No. 73 Squadron.
15. Letter from Ronald Adam to the author.
16. Ibid.
17. Public Record Office, Richthofen Combat Reports; Sopwith F.1 Camel D.6439 of No. 3 Squadron, Maj Richard Raymond-Barker, MC, aged 23 (KiA).
18. Bodenschatz, op. cit., p. 80.
19. Richthofen, M. von. *Der rote Kampfflieger* (1933 edn.), pp. 203–4.
20. Quoted in *Ein Heldenleben*, op. cit., p. 261.
21. Quoted in Flanagan, B. 'Lieut. Wilfrid "Wop" May's Account', in

Cross & Cockade Journal, 1982, p. 112.

22. No. 209 Squadron Combat Report of 2/Lt W. R. May in Sopwith F.1 Camel D.3326.

23. No. 209 Squadron Combat Report of Lt F. J. W. Mellersh in Sopwith F.1 Camel B.6257.

24. No. 209 Squadron Combat Report of Capt A. R. Brown in Sopwith F.1 Camel B.7270.

25. *Nachrichtenblatt*, Nr. 13, 23 May 1918, p. 193.

26. Hoeppner, E. von. *Deutschlands Krieg in der Luft*, p. 157.

27. Quoted in McGuire, F. (ed.). 'Documents Relating to Richthofen's Last Battle', in *Over the Front*, 1987, p. 172.

28. Ibid., p. 170.

29. Douglas, W. S. *Years of Combat*, p. 305.

30. Ibid., p. 306.

31. Quoted in Richthofen, op. cit., p. 261.

32. Ibid., pp. 261–2.

33. Hook, J., 'A Visit to the Richthofen Museum', in *Popular Flying*, 1934, p. 534.

34. Ibid., p. 564.

Appendix I

1. Richthofen, M. von. *Der rote Kampfflieger* (1917 edn.), pp. 55, 61–2.

2. Ibid., pp. 50–1.

3. Supf, P., *Das Buch der deutschen Fluggeschichte*, vol. II, p. 504.

4. Immelmann, F. *Immelmann – 'Der Adler von Lille'*, p. 93.

5. Ibid., p. 80.

6. Böhme, E., *Briefe eines deutschen Kampffliegers an ein junges Mädchen*, pp. 69–70.

7. Krefft, K. *Kriegsranglisten-Auszug*, pp. 2–3.

8. Quoted in Schnitzler, E. *Carl Allmenröder der bergische Kampfflieger*, p. 9.

9. Quoted in Zuerl, W. *Pour le Mérite-Flieger*, p. 480.

10. Schäfer, K. *Vom Jäger zum Flieger*, pp. 93–4.

11. Quoted in Schmeelke, M. 'Leutnant der Reserve Otto Brauneck' Part II, in *Over the Front*, 1986, p. 198.

12. Richthofen, op. cit., pp. 166–7.

13. Quoted from a letter to the von Falkenhayn family via a private source.

14. Bufe, O. *Kriegsranglisten-Auszug*, pp. 2–4.

15. Quoted in Zuerl, op. cit., p. 535.

16. Ibid., pp. 315–17.

17. Richthofen, L. von. 'Das letzte Mal in der Luft', in *Im Felde unbesiegt*, p. 288.

18. Hildebrand, H. *Die Generale der deutschen Luftwaffe*, vol. II, p. 180.

19. Quoted in Zuerl, op. cit., p. 267.

20. O'Connor, N. *Aviation Awards of Imperial Germany in World War I*, vol. II, p. 219.

21. For details, see Kilduff, P. *The Red Baron Combat Wing*, pp. 128–9.

22. Richthofen, K. von. *Mein Kriegstagebuch*, p. 133.

23. Zuerl, op. cit., p. 449.

24. This rating is based on new research in Shores, C., Franks, N., and Guest, R. *Above the Trenches*, pp. 255–6, which adjusts the long-held score of Major Edward Mannock, VC, from 73 to 62 confirmed victories.

25. Hildebrand, H. *Die Generale der deutschen Luftwaffe*, vol. III, pp. 420–1.

26. Quoted in Richthofen, M. von. *Ein Heldenleben*, pp. 261–2.

Bibliography

Books

Bartlett, C. *Bomber Pilot 1916–1918*. London, 1974

Bodenschatz, K. *Jagd in Flanderns Himmel – Aus den sechzen Kampfmonaten des Jagdgeschwaders Freiherr von Richthofen*. Munich, 1935

Böhme, E. *Briefe eines deutschen Kampffliegers an ein junges Mädchen*. Leipzig, 1930

Boelcke, O. *Hauptmann Boelckes Feldberichte*. Gotha, 1916

Bruce, J. *British Aeroplanes 1914–1918*. London, 1969

Burge, C. *The Annals of 100 Squadron*. London, c. 1919

Douglas, W. S. *Years of Combat*. London, 1963

Flipts, A., Faillie, M., and Faillie, R. *Marke Wereldoorlog I*. Marke, 1984

Franks, N., Bailey, F., and Guest, R. *Above the Lines*. London, 1993

Franks, N., Giblin, H., and McCrery, N. *Under the Guns of the Red Baron*. London, 1995

Franks, N., Bailey F., and Duiven, R. *The Jasta Pilots*. London, 1996

Für Tapferkeit und Verdienst. Munich, 1956

Gibbons, F. *The Red Knight of Germany*. New York, 1927

Haythornthwaite, P. *The World War One Source Book*. London, 1994

Henshaw, T. *The Sky Their Battlefield*. London, 1995.

Hildebrand, H. *Die Generale der deutschen Luftwaffe 1935–1945*. Osnabrück, vol. II, 1991; vol. III, 1992

Hobson, C. *Airmen Died in the Great War 1914–1918*. London, 1995

Hoeppner, E. von. *Deutschlands Krieg in der Luft*. Leipzig, 1921

Immelmann, F. (ed.). *Immelmann – 'Der Adler von Lille'*. Leipzig, 1934

Immelmann, M. *Meine Kampfflüge*. Berlin, 1916

Jones, H. A. *The War in the Air*. Oxford, vol. IV, 1934

Kilduff, P. *Germany's First Air Force 1914–1918*. London, 1991

– *Richthofen – Beyond the Legend of the Red Baron*. London, 1993

– *The Red Baron Combat Wing*. London, 1997

Lamberton, W. *Fighter Aircraft of the 1914–1918 War*. Letchworth, 1960

Malkowsky, E. *Vom Heldenkampf der deutschen Flieger*. Berlin, 1917.

Morris, A. *Bloody April*. London, 1967

Nowarra, H., and Brown, K. *Von Richthofen and the Flying Circus*. Letchworth, 1964

O'Connor, N. *Aviation Awards of Imperial Germany in World War I and the Men Who Earned Them*. Princeton, vol. II *Kingdom of Prussia*, 1990

Perthes, J. *Ehrentafel des reichsdeutschen Adels 1914–1919*. Gotha, 1921

Richthofen, K. von. *Mein Kriegstagebuch*. Berlin, 1937

Richthofen, M. von. *Ein Heldenleben*. Berlin, 1920

– *Der rote Kampfflieger*. Berlin, 1917, 1933

Robertson, B. *British Military Aircraft Serials 1911–1971*. Shepperton, 1971

Schäfer, K. *Vom Jäger zum Flieger*. Berlin, 1917

Shores, C., Franks, N., and Guest, R. *Above the Trenches*. London, 1990

Supf, P. *Das Buch der deutschen Fluggeschichte*. Stuttgart, vol. II, 1958

Udet, E. *Mein Fliegerleben*. Berlin, 1935

Van Ishoven, A. (ed, C. Bowyer). *The Fall of an Eagle*. London, 1977

Wenzl, R. *Richthofen-Flieger*. Freiburg im Breisgau, c.1930

Zuerl, W. *Pour le Mérite-Flieger*. Munich, 1938

Documents

Idflieg, *Jagdgeschwader I Erfahrungsaustausch*. Charlottenburg, 1918

Kogenluft, *Nachrichtenblatt der Luftstreitkräfte*. Berlin, vol. 1, 1917; vol. 2, 1918

Kommandeur der Flieger der 4. Armee Wochenberichte, 1917

Stabsoffizier der Flieger der 1. Armee Wochenberichte, 1916

Stabsoffizier/Kommandeur der Flieger der 6. Armee Wochenberichte, 1916, 1917

Richthofen combat reports (trans.), Public Record Office, London, n.d. (PRO File Air 1/686/21/13/2250 XC15183)

Royal Flying Corps/Royal Air Force:

Communiqués from the field, 1917, 1918 (PRO Air 1/2097/207/14/1)

No. 25 Squadron combat reports, 1917 (PRO Air 1/1221/204/5/2634/25 Sqn)

No. 29 Squadron combat reports, 1917 (PRO Air 1/1221/204/5/2634/29 Sqn)

No. 32 Squadron record book, 1917 (PRO Air 1/1493/204/38/3)

No. 40 Squadron combat reports, 1917 (PRO Air 1/204/5/2634/40 Sqn)

No. 46 Squadron record book, 1917

(PRO Air 1/1426/204/31/7)
No. 48 Squadron combat reports, 1918 (PRO Air 1/1223/204/5/2634/48 Sqn)
No. 73 Squadron combat reports, 1918 (PRO Air 1/1226/204/5/2534/73 Sqn)
No. 209 Squadron combat reports, 1918 (PRO Air 1/2222/209/40/17)
RFC, *Periodical Summary of Aeronautical Information*, Nos. 1–30. In the field, 22 May 1917 – 11 February 1918
– *Summaries of Air Intelligence*, Nos. 1 – 263. In the field, 12 February – 11 November 1918
War Diary, in the field, 1917 (PRO Air 1/1184-1188/204/5/2595)
Western Front Casualty List, in the field, 1917, 1918 (PRO Air 1/967/204/5/1097-969/204/5/1102)

Articles, Monographs and Periodicals

Bailey, F., Duiven, R., and Manning, R., 'A Short History of No. 62 Squadron, RFC/RAF', in *Cross & Cockade Journal*, 1976
Baron, G. *Schlesische Flieger Nachrichten*. Bielefeld, 1986
Ferko, A. E., *Richthofen*. Berkhamsted, 1995
Flanagan, B. 'Lieut. Wilfrid "Wop" May's Account', in *Cross & Cockade Journal*, 1982
Flashar, R. 'In der Tankschlacht von Cambrai', in Neumann, G. (ed.).

In der Luft unbesiegt. Munich, 1923
'Führende Männer im Weltkrieg – General von Lossberg' in *Kriegs-Echo*, Nr. 166. Berlin, 1917
'Führende Männer im Weltkrieg – General d.I. Sixt von Arnim' in *Kriegs-Echo*, Nr. 185. Berlin, 1917
Garwood, J. 'The Survivors', in *Cross & Cockade Journal*, 1961
G. G. 'Führende Männer im Weltkrieg – Fliegerhauptmann Boelcke', in *Kriegs-Echo*, Nr. 118. Berlin, 1916
Grosz, P. 'The Agile and Aggressive Albatros', in *Air Enthusiast*, No. 1, 1976
Grosz, P., and Ferko, A. E. 'Fokker Dr.I – Reappraisal', in *Air Enthusiast*, No. 8, 1978
Grosz, P., and Schneide, K. 'Historiography: Cockburn-Lange', in *WW I Aero*, No. 102, 1984
Hook, J. 'A Visit to the Richthofen Museum', in *Popular Flying*, 1934
Kriegs-Echo Wochen-Chronik. Berlin, 1917.
Lampel, P. 'Als Gast beim Rittmeister Frhr. v.Richthofen', in Neumann, G. (ed.). *In der Luft unbesiegt*. Munich, 1923
McGuire, F. (ed.). 'Documents Relating to Richthofen's Last Battle', in *Over the Front*. 1987
Nowarra, H. 'A Bomber Chief and a Fighter Pilot – Two Interviews',

in *Cross & Cockade Journal*, 1960
Osten, H-G. von der (ed. L. Zacharias). 'Memoirs of World War I with Jagdstaffeln 11 and 4', in *Cross & Cockade Journal*, 1974
Radloff, B., and Niemann, R. 'The Ehrenbechers – Where Are They Now?', in *Cross & Cockade Journal*, 1969
Richthofen, L. von. 'Das letzte Mal an der Front, Juli – August 1918', in Dickhuth-Harrach, G. von (ed.). *Im Felde unbesiegt*, vol. I. Munich, 1921
Salzmann, E. von. 'Führende Männer im Weltkrieg – Erich von Falkenhayn', in *Kriegs-Echo*, Nr. 75. Berlin, 1916
Schmeelke, M. 'Leutnant der Reserve Otto Brauneck' Part II, in *Over the Front*. 1986
Schnitzler, E. *Carl Allmenröder der bergische Kampfflieger*. Wald, 1927
W. H., 'Führende Männer im Weltkrieg – Reichskanzler Dr. Michaelis', in *Kriegs-Echo*, Nr. 155. Berlin, 1917

Other Sources

Adam, R. Correspondence
Bufe, O. *Kriegsrangenlist-Auszug*. 1919
Falkenhayn, F. von. Correspondence
Krefft, K. *Kriegsrangenlist-Auszug*. 1919
Reinhard, W. *Personal-Bogen*. 1918

Index

MILITARY FORMATIONS, ETC.

Air Staffs, German Army
Kommandeur der Flieger der 2. Armee, 36
Kommandeur der Flieger der 4. Armee, 76, 77, 83, 136
Kommandeur der Flieger der 6. Armee, 47, 55, 64, 136
Kommandeur der Flieger der 8. Armee, 137

Air Units, British/Commonwealth:
No. 1 Squadron, RFC, 152
No. 2 Squadron, RFC, 52
No. 3 Squadron, AFC, 120, 122
No. 3 Squadron, RAF, 153
No. 5 Squadron, RNAS, 153
No. 6 Squadron, RFC, 152
No. 7 Squadron, RFC, 84
No. 8 Squadron, RNAS, 52, 151
No. 11 Squadron, RFC, 53, 150, 153
No. 12 Squadron, RFC, 52, 151
No. 13 Squadron, RFC, 51, 52, 151
No. 16 Squadron, RFC, 21, 54
No. 19 Squadron, RFC, 39, 52, 56, 82, 83, 134, 151, 152
No. 20 Squadron, RFC, 75
No. 21 Squadron, RFC, 52
No. 24 Squadron, RFC, 32, 150, 153
No. 25 Squadron, RFC, 34, 52, 54, 151, 155
No. 29 Squadron, RFC, 52, 67, 152, 155
No. 32 Squadron, RFC, 39, 52, 76, 150, 155
No. 40 Squadron, RFC, 35, 150, 155
No. 41 Squadron, RFC, 153
No. 43 Squadron, RFC, 52, 150, 151
No. 44 Squadron, RFC, 116
No. 46 Squadron, RFC, 153, 155
No. 48 Squadron, RFC, 52, 53, 104, 153, 155

No. 52 Squadron, RFC, 153
No. 53 Squadron, RFC, 72
No. 54 Squadron, RFC, 153
No. 56 Squadron, RFC, 139
No. 57 Squadron, RFC, 152
No. 59 Squadron, RFC, 48, 53
No. 60 Squadron, RFC, 45, 151
No. 62 Squadron, RFC, 104, 105, 153, 155
No. 64 Squadron, RFC, 95
No. 65 Squadron, RFC, 94
No. 70 Squadron, RFC, 150
No. 73 Squadron, RFC/RAF, 106, 116, 153, 155
No. 84 Squadron, RAF, 122
No. 100 Squadron, RFC, 44, 151
No. 209 Squadron, RAF, 118, 119, 122, 154, 155

Air Units, German:
Brieftauben-Abteilung Ostende, 14, 15, 16, 17, 31, 66, 92, 129
Feldflieger-Abteilung 1b, 136
Feldflieger-Abteilung 5b, 132
Feldflieger-Abteilung 18, 33, 64, 132–133
Feldflieger-Abteilung 20, 130
Feldflieger-Abteilung 22, 28
Feldflieger-Abteilung 62, 130, 131
Feldflieger-Abteilung 69, 14, 129
Flieger-Abteilung (A) 206, 140
Flieger-Abteilung (A) 227, 133
Flieger-Abteilung (A) 258, 38
Flieger-Abteilung (A) 265, 138
Flieger-Ersatz-Abteilung 6, 14
Flieger-Ersatz-Abteilung 7, 13, 63
Flieger-Ersatz-Abteilung 9, 140
Jagdgeschwader I, 70, 71, 73–84, 92–94, 96, 98, 99, 103, 104, 106, 107, 108, 110–114, 116–118, 120, 127, 132, 137, 139
Jagdgeschwader II, 127
Jagdgruppe 2, 108

Jagdstaffel 2, 24, 25, 26, 27, 32, 39, 42, 78, 132, 139
Jagdstaffel 3, 67
Jagdstaffel 4, 47, 48, 51, 70, 73, 75, 77, 80, 99, 103, 104, 112, 113, 127, 137, 138, 140, 152
Jagdstaffel 5, 94, 106, 108
Jagdstaffel 6, 34, 70, 73, 75, 79, 82, 97, 99, 103, 108, 110, 114, 116, 137
Jagdstaffel 10, 70, 73, 84, 95, 99, 100, 103, 104, 110, 137, 138, 139
Jagdstaffel 11, 33–36, 41, 43–48, 50, 51, 54, 55, 58, 59, 67, 69, 70, 73, 75, 76, 79, 80, 81, 85, 93, 94, 95, 96, 97, 99, 101, 102, 103, 107, 110, 112, 113, 114, 116, 117, 132–137, 140
Jagdstaffel 12, 49
Jagdstaffel 15, 93, 94, 140
Jagdstaffel 25, 135
Jagdstaffel 26, 101
Jagdstaffel 28w, 55, 67
Jagdstaffel 29, 78
Jagdstaffel 30, 66
Jagdstaffel 37, 107, 108, 140
Jagdstaffel 46, 108
Kampfeinsitzer-Kommando III, 132
Kampfeinsitzer-Kommando Habsheim, 140
Kampfgeschwader 1, 23, 92
Kampfgeschwader 2, 18, 22, 23, 24, 90, 132
Kampfgeschwader 3, 92
Kampfgeschwader 4, 36, 136
Kampfstaffel 8, 19, 108
Kampfstaffel 23, 136
II. Marine-Feldflieger-Abteilung, 71

Army Units, Formations and Facilities: Austro-Hungarian
6. Armeekorps, 14

157